Design Thinking

Design Thinking is a set of strategic and creative processes and principles used in the planning and creation of products and solutions to human-centered design problems.

With design and innovation being two key driving principles, this series focuses on, but is not limited to, the following areas and topics:

- User Interface (UI) and User Experience (UX) Design

- Psychology of Design

- Human-Computer Interaction (HCI)

- Ergonomic Design

- Product Development and Management

- Virtual and Mixed Reality (VR/XR)

- User-Centered Built Environments and Smart Homes

- Accessibility, Sustainability and Environmental Design

- Learning and Instructional Design

- Strategy and best practices

This series publishes books aimed at designers, developers, storytellers and problem-solvers in industry to help them understand current developments and best practices at the cutting edge of creativity, to invent new paradigms and solutions, and challenge Creatives to push boundaries to design bigger and better than before.

More information about this series at https://link.springer.com/bookseries/15933.

Beginning Voice Search Optimization

An Introductory Toolkit to Voice-Driven SEO

Alex Libby

Apress®

Beginning Voice Search Optimization: An Introductory Toolkit to Voice-Driven SEO

Alex Libby
Belper, Derbyshire, UK

ISBN-13 (pbk): 979-8-8688-1840-0 ISBN-13 (electronic): 979-8-8688-1841-7
https://doi.org/10.1007/979-8-8688-1841-7

Copyright © 2025 by Alex Libby

Managing Director, Apress Media LLC: Welmoed Spahr
Acquisitions Editor: James Robinson-Prior
Editorial Assistant: Jacob Shmulewitz

Cover designed by eStudioCalamar

Distributed to the book trade worldwide by Springer Science+Business Media New York, 1 New York Plaza, New York, NY 10004. Phone 1-800-SPRINGER, fax (201) 348-4505, e-mail orders-ny@springer-sbm.com, or visit www.springeronline.com. Apress Media, LLC is a Delaware LLC and the sole member (owner) is Springer Science + Business Media Finance Inc (SSBM Finance Inc). SSBM Finance Inc is a **Delaware** corporation.

For information on translations, please e-mail booktranslations@springernature.com; for reprint, paperback, or audio rights, please e-mail bookpermissions@springernature.com.

Apress titles may be purchased in bulk for academic, corporate, or promotional use. eBook versions and licenses are also available for most titles. For more information, reference our Print and eBook Bulk Sales web page at http://www.apress.com/bulk-sales.

Any source code or other supplementary material referenced by the author in this book is available to readers on GitHub. For more detailed information, please visit https://www.apress.com/gp/services/source-code.

If disposing of this product, please recycle the paper

This is dedicated to my family, with thanks for their love and support while writing this book.

Table of Contents

About the Author

Alex Libby is a front-end developer and seasoned computer book author, who hails from England. His passion for all things open source dates back to his student days, when he first came across web development, and has been hooked ever since. When he's not writing code for frontend features as part of his normal work, Alex enjoys tinkering with different open source libraries to see how they work. He has spent a stint maintaining the jQuery Tools library and enjoys writing about open source technologies, principally for front-end UI development.

About the Technical Reviewer

 **Vadim Atamanenko** is a seasoned software engineer with over 20 years of experience in designing and delivering complex systems across industries such as finance, insurance, and public services. He has developed solutions that have helped thousands of users streamline operations and eliminate manual processes.

Vadim is an active participant in the global tech community – he frequently serves as a judge and mentor at international hackathons and regularly speaks at IT conferences. He is a member of the IEEE (Institute of Electrical and Electronics Engineers) and the Harvard Square Business Association.

Currently, he serves as Chief Information Officer at Freedom Holding Corp., where he leads digital transformation initiatives. He enjoys meeting new people and sharing knowledge.

Feel free to connect with him on LinkedIn: linkedin.com/in/vadim-atamanenko.

Acknowledgments

Writing a book can be a long but rewarding process – I still remember starting to write my first book back in 2011, which seems such a long time ago!

Whatever the size or nature of any book, it is not possible to complete it without the help of other people. To that end, I would like to offer a huge vote of thanks to my editors – in particular, Sowmya Thodur and James Robinson-Prior; my thanks also to Vadim Atamanenko as my technical reviewer, James Markham for his help during the process, and others at Apress for getting this book into print. All have made writing this book a painless and enjoyable process, even with the edits!

My thanks also to my family for being understanding and supporting me while writing. I frequently spend a lot of late nights writing alone, or pass up times when I should be with them, so their words of encouragement and support have been a real help in getting past those bumps in the road and producing the finished book that you now hold in your hands.

Introduction

Beginning Voice Search Optimization is for people who want to learn how to quickly implement voice search optimization (or VSO), with the minimum of effort and tools.

This project-oriented book first examines what the VSO is all about, the benefits of using it, and touch on where it fits into the landscape as a complement to standard SEO practice. We'll examine the various parts of VSO and understand how we can implement it quickly with existing tools available in your project, using React and Next.js as our example framework.

Throughout this book, I'll take you on a journey through implementing VSO, exploring how not only is it important for developers to be involved, but that the principles of VSO extend to others such as UX designers and stakeholders, showing that we all have a part to play in the success of our website. We'll start with the basic concepts behind VSO, some of the challenges we'll face, and why it plays such an important role. We'll also take a look at how to deal with voice when implementing VSO, plus topics such as recognizing your location automatically (and adapting features to suit), as well as how we can easily make changes with tools that already exist in the browser, as a precursor to developing something more complex over time.

VSO is still a relatively new topic, so there are unknowns – I'll help pinpoint what you need to look out for, so you can start transitioning to using VSO and make your content available for all manner of devices. With this book, you'll get a good grounding in the principles of VSO, using tools you already possess, so you can begin to develop your VSO strategy in your future projects.

CHAPTER 1

Getting Started

"Alexa, what time is it, please?"

"Good afternoon, Alex. The time is two twenty-nine pm..."

Does this sound familiar?

Cast your mind back a few years when voice-driven smart assistants (the likes of Alexa and friends) first came out – it felt a little weird at the time, but yes, you could ask a small plastic device to tell you the time anywhere in the world, give you the latest news headlines, and more. While Alexa has only been around since 2013, the technology behind what we know as speech recognition dates back as far as … yes, 1952!

Now, let's switch to something completely different: I want you to try a quick test for me based on searching for how to make one of my favorite drinks.

HOW TO MAKE A CAPPUCCINO

For this demo, we'll use Google – I'll assume you will use the US site at `https://www.google.com`:

1. Crack open your browser of choice, then head over to Google.

2. Enter this search phrase: "How do I make a cappuccino" (no quotes), into the search box, and press Enter.

© Alex Libby 2025
A. Libby, *Beginning Voice Search Optimization*, Design Thinking,
https://doi.org/10.1007/979-8-8688-1841-7_1

3. If all is well, you should see the result shown in Figure 1-1.

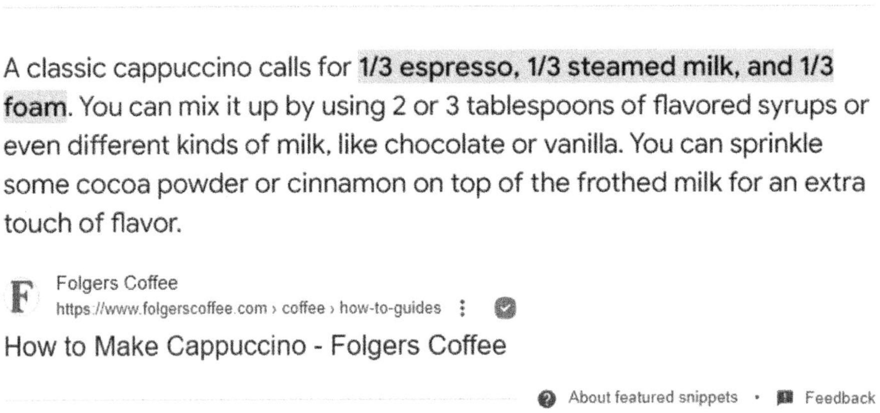

A classic cappuccino calls for **1/3 espresso, 1/3 steamed milk, and 1/3 foam**. You can mix it up by using 2 or 3 tablespoons of flavored syrups or even different kinds of milk, like chocolate or vanilla. You can sprinkle some cocoa powder or cinnamon on top of the frothed milk for an extra touch of flavor.

F Folgers Coffee
https://www.folgerscoffee.com › coffee › how-to-guides ⋮   ☑

How to Make Cappuccino - Folgers Coffee

❓ About featured snippets • 📕 Feedback

Figure 1-1. *Results of our question to Google*

Okay, so this book isn't about how to make a beverage based on one of the most popular drinks worldwide (two billion cups a day!), but in this case, I want to highlight two critical words at the bottom right of that last image that form a small part of the focus of this book: **featured snippets**.

It's important to note that you may or may not get an AI-generated response as well – this will usually come before the featured snippets response and should not be confused with them. Look for the description at the bottom of each section for the right response.

Now, I suspect you're wondering what searching for coffee and using smart assistants have in common, and more to the point, why I started this chapter with two seemingly unrelated topics! Fear not, my dear readers – let me explain everything. Welcome to voice search optimization (VSO).

Introducing VSO

Let's step back for a moment to something I'm sure you'll have come across, at least in passing.

As a developer, I'm sure you will be familiar with the term search engine optimization in some form or other – granted, it might not be with the fine-tuning of keywords and more to do with implementing the basic framework.

The basic premise is to improve the amount and quality of unpaid or organic traffic to your website so there is less need for paid traffic. To achieve this, we (as a company) have to work on producing quality content and backlinks while making sure that the site speed is good, that the links on our site are still valid, and so on.

While this will all help, the net result is that we still have to search using keywords we type into Google – it's solid and works(-ish). But it is a step that hasn't changed in over 20 years – at least not until now. Imagine what if we could search for content in Google, or even on our site, and find results … *using our voice?* Yes, you heard me right – welcome to the world of voice search optimization.

So, what is this all about? Well, it's not any single technology but more a set of principles we should follow if we want to enable our site for voice, particularly when searching for content. Almost 20% of all searches are conducted by voice – expectations are that this will increase dramatically within the next couple of years, if not sooner. Early incarnations of voice search tools were – shall we say – a little temperamental: thanks to advances in AI, tools such as Google's voice search have massively improved. Indeed, Google boasts a 95% accuracy rate, with a word error percentage lower than 5%!

It might all sound a little wild, but it makes sense if you think about it. To understand why, let's first dive in and take a closer look at how it works, before we explore the importance of implementing VSO to your site.

Exploring How VSO Works

Let's, for argument's sake, say you decided you want to get a pizza online – you happen to have just moved home, and are not familiar with the area. You fancy a pizza – there's a good chance you will likely use Google to find out – "pizza near me" should bring up some options, as shown in Figure 1-2.

Q   pizza near me delivery   ✕   🎤   📷

Q   pizza near me delivery

Q   pizza near me delivery **now**

Q   pizza near me delivery **within 1 mi**

Q   pizza near me delivery **within 0.5 mi**

Q   pizza near me delivery **within 0.2 mi**

Q   pizza near me delivery **open now 24 hours**

Figure 1-2. *Finding a local pizzeria for takeout*

Notice how it's showing multiple entries that are very similar? It is another small part of VSO, where it works out different options that could apply based on your request. These queries work okay, but we can do better! Now imagine that you asked it verbally to search: instead of getting dozens of results, you will get a more concise set of results from outlets selling pizza near you. In this case, search engines such as Google use a four-step process to get those results.

In this list, I'm using voice assistant as a generic reference to any device that can interpret and recognize spoken text and transform it into a written equivalent.

1. After articulating the request, the first step is filtering out background noise – a voice assistant mutes any background noise, so picking up only your voice.

2. It then digitizes the voice search query, which turns the sound waves that form your query into digital data. It uses an extensive database to turn that digital data into digital text data.

3. At this stage, nothing has been done with the text per se; this comes next. The search assistant now analyzes the voice query to process the digital data before connecting to external sources to find relevant answers and match the query with the most relevant content using search algorithms.

4. As the last step, voice assistants will recognize query patterns, compare them to their database, and adapt to specific voice and language patterns. In future requests, it will help improve the accuracy and relevance of the responses.

To understand how this fits together, I've put together an image showing how a request from your site would be transformed into a response shown in the browser (Figure 1-3).

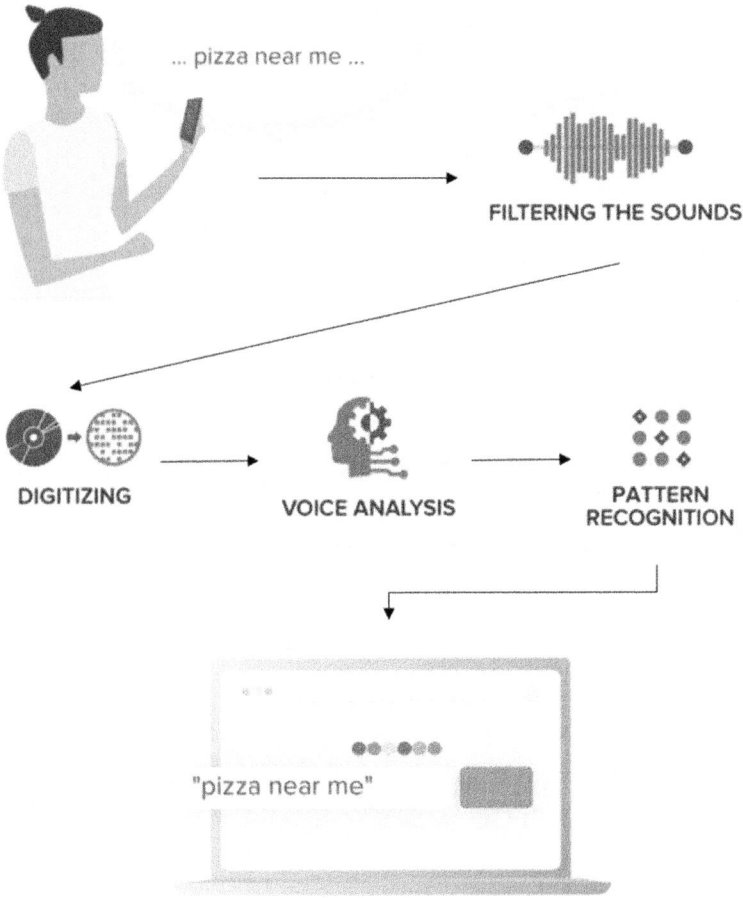

Figure 1-3. *The process for searching by voice (Source: digitalguider.com)*

Although I've used "pizza near me," speech recognition should recognize any content we throw at it. There are some potential challenges we may face with this, though, such as dialects and regional differences – I'll come back to this later in this chapter when we look at some of the challenges we might face with VSO.

To fully use speech recognition, though, we need to adapt how we articulate the queries – phrases such as those shown in Figure 1-2 won't be enough. Instead, we have to move to using more natural language queries. I make no apology: you'll see this pop up time and time again!

It is part of what makes VSO different, though, and something I am sure will come up in conversations with stakeholders. So, to get us ahead of the game, let's dive in and take a look at this in more detail.

Why Is Voice Search Different?

So, why is voice search different? In answer, it all boils down to one word – alignment.

We'll always work on tasks that would equally apply to both transitional SEO as well as VSO, but when it comes to VSO, the critical difference is *how* we articulate the requests – instead of using short phrases of 1-3 words, for example, we will use longer phrases and even short sentences as queries. Think back to that screenshot in Figure 1-2 – we'd need to rephrase that as a question more aligned with how we think and communicate with others.

It isn't the only way that voice search optimization (VSO) and traditional SEO differ – I've some key differences in Table 1-1.

Table 1-1. *Key differences between VSO and traditional SEO*

Area	Traditional SEO	Voice Search Optimization
Content	Focuses on optimizing content for text-based searches	Focuses on optimizing content for spoken queries
Language	Tend to be short text-based queries, such as "best restaurants in Manhattan"	Voice search queries are more conversational and natural – similar to "What are the best restaurants near me?"
Length/ keywords	Typically short queries	Voice search queries tend to be longer and more complex, favoring longtail keywords that contain more than three words
Local optimization	We can do this as part of SEO, but probably not with the same level of focus – it tends to be more toward getting higher in the results!	It plays a more prominent role in VSO, which tends to see fewer results, but results are of higher quality and relevance to the user
Intent	Traditional SEO queries can't interpret intent, so results tend to be based on where there is a pattern match	Engines can better interpret intent from voice queries and deliver more focused/ accurate results
Natural Language Processing (NLP)	Traditional queries tend to be shorter phrases that are not natural language, so NLP doesn't play a role – results in a broader range of answers, not necessarily of as good quality or relevance as VSO	NLP is a key element of VSO, allowing search engines to understand and analyze human language

These differences are just something to think about – we'll touch on them throughout this book. The critical point here is that alignment is more to how we as humans speak; it makes it easier to determine what content to use and queries to create, rather than creating a random mix of keywords for SEO and hoping they produce some form of result.

Cast your mind back to Figure 1-2, where I deliberately chose "pizza near me delivery" as a search term, not because I was hungry(!), but to illustrate the kind of command we would typically enter into Google to perform that search. The term we used works to an extent, but if we apply the concepts listed in the second column of Table 1-1, we can see how VSO will help improve the accuracy, natural feel, and relevance of any query we use.

The important takeaway for anyone implementing VSO is to forget everything they've done and start again. This statement may sound a little radical, particularly as some of what we would do for SEO would equally apply to VSO. However, gone are the days of thinking we need to speak Googlese (as some of my friends used to say!) and instead think in more natural terms, more akin to how we operate.

To put this into context, Figure 1-4 shows a more natural form of query as an example, this time for making savory cakes.

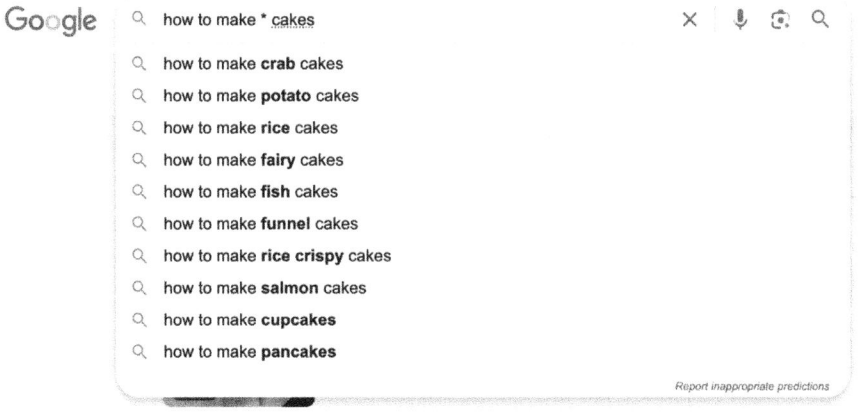

Figure 1-4. A natural language query in Google

At first glance, this would be much easier for customers, as they say what they think, not a random mix of words that doesn't make sense! Entering something more aligned with how we think removes some of the effort required by customers and returns more relevant results.

We may only get a fraction of the results we might otherwise have had with a traditional query, but that doesn't matter – these results will be more accurate and relevant, as shown by this chart from the Digital Guider website, which illustrates what happens when you use more words in your query (Figure 1-5).

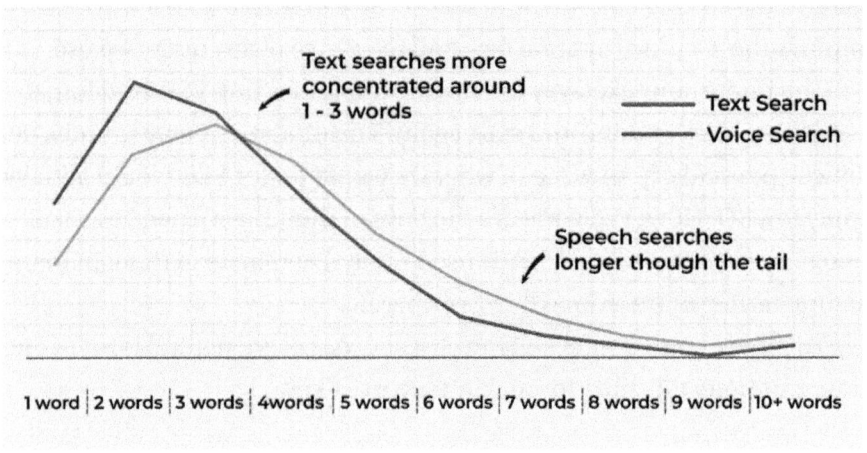

Figure 1-5. *A chart illustrating the use of more words to refine speech results*
(Source: Digital Guider website)

The point here is that in an age of voice-activated search, we need to be on top of our game when optimizing our content for voice-driven searches – the number of people searching this way will only increase!

If you would like to learn more about why smaller numbers of results are better, it has much to do with the recent Hummingbird and BERT algorithm upgrades done by Google. This change switched attention to searcher intent by identifying the underlying meaning of queries (rather than just the specific terms in a query) and offering more relevant results to more conversational voice inquiries. This change made searching faster, as it returns a smaller number of more relevant results, which reduces the risk of feeling overwhelmed!

Okay – let's crack on. So far, we've covered what VSO is, how it works (at a high level), and why it differs from SEO. We still need to answer one burning question: Why is it important to implement VSO, and how does it affect us?

Understanding the Importance of VSO

So, how do we answer this question? Well, remember that at the start of this chapter, I touched on how so many people are now using voice (or smart) assistants worldwide – to give you some idea, 50% of adults worldwide now use one in some form each day!

Owners use their smart devices to perform tasks such as searching for information or comparing prices – this means we have a huge market to tap into for VSO! The benefits alone outweigh the resources and effort required to implement it on our sites:

- Increasing the number of voice search results on our site will increase brand awareness, especially at the local level in your community or region.

- Making content available through voice helps to build trust with your local audience, as they will see your business providing valuable and trustworthy information.

- Implementing options to optimize for voice will improve SEO, leading to an improved user experience – voice search requires a different set of queries but in a format more closely aligned to how we think, rather than second-guess what keywords we need to use to find something in Google.

We can see some examples of how people use their devices in Figure 1-6. Granted, the data may be a bit old, but the principle still applies.

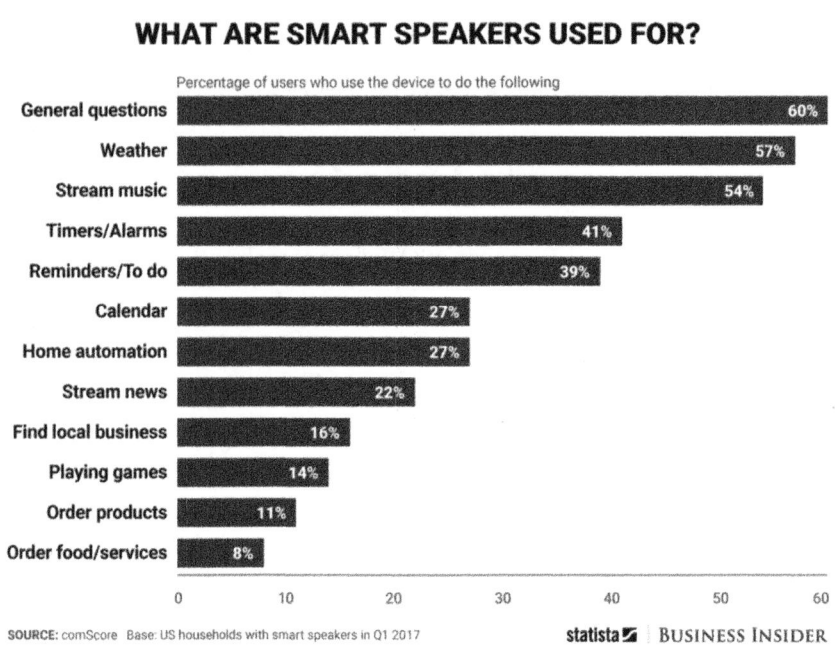

Figure 1-6. *A chart to illustrate the types of usage for smart assistants (Source: voicebot.ai website)*

Reflect for a moment on the search we performed earlier for instructions on making a cappuccino. Imagine if you performed an identical search as we did earlier, but this time from a smart assistant.

There's every chance you will get the same results recited back to you and from the same site – imagine if it could be yours?

Featured snippets are one of several ways we can implement voice search optimization on our site. Granted, we may not be able to control when or how often Google uses them, but that *almost* doesn't matter – the benefits outweigh the time and resources needed to implement VSO on our sites. But bear in mind that there is every possibility that the results we get could easily come from your site, all as a result of implementing the featured snippets we mentioned just now.

These benefits we talked about just now are just a fraction of what VSO can offer – a less obvious one, for example, is accessibility. As long as someone has a working microphone and we build an appropriate UI, there is no need to use mice or keyboards – this would suit anyone who might use a wheelchair with limited mobility. Sure, we can still use text search if we need to, but it's very old school – VSO is a great way to not only make our site more accessible but also bring using it up to modern-day methods and potentially make it easier for a broader audience to use.

Okay, let's move on: so far, we've talked about what VSO is, how it works, and the importance of using it on our site. It's time to bring things closer to home – if we start to use it, we need to prepare ourselves for a wholesale shift in our mindset; this change **will affect everybody**. And yes, I do mean everyone...

Changing Behaviors and Expectations

If someone asked you to sum up what you had to do in one word when talking about VSO, it's pretty safe to say that word could be "adapt."

At first, this might sound odd, but think about it for a second – as developers, product owners, or SEO experts, we've all been used to knowing the importance of optimizing our site for SEO. VSO uses a lot of the same principles (at least from a developer's perspective), but in a new way; some of the tasks we have to do (such as optimizing for speed), we still need to do, but there are extra tasks such as putting together natural language queries and adapting our interface so it's accessible by voice only.

The best way to think about it is to imagine you can't touch your keyboard or mouse and have someone controlling them for you. Instead of you being in *direct* control, you have to articulate your commands to someone else who is steering for you!

Try it out on your website – let me guess, it's more complicated than you think!

Adapting any site for VSO enforces the need for a whole new mindset – there are a few things to think about:

- The role of research plays a super critical part in VSO: it's always important, but it becomes even more so when referring to VSO.

- It's super important for developers to have a mindset that puts customers first – not just from a usability perspective but also from what questions they ask, how they search, and so on. It's a great skill to have, but it won't come easily for everyone!

- I've touched on how people use the likes of Alexa or Siri to perform research. We need to ask ourselves how much we want to expose to voice search or whether our content is suitable for us to do this.

14

I'm assuming that by reading this book, there is a desire to make content available as a principle, but at the same time, we need to make sure it's appropriate to do so – we don't want to expose confidential information or content that could cause legal issues!

- We also need to look at analytics in detail: what terms do people use now? Bear in mind that these terms could still be usable going forward, but we need to shift to a mindset where people can ask natural-language questions rather than cobble together several words and hope that they produce the desired results. It will not happen overnight, but we can transition over time with careful research.

Although implementing VSO will take a website to a new level, it does present unique challenges for developers. A key part of these challenges lies around the need to adapt websites to accommodate the nuances of spoken language and user behavior. It's easier to see now that we take for granted a lot when it comes to operating websites – let's have a look at some of these challenges in more detail.

Challenges in Providing VSO

When implementing VSO, you might first think that the following list will look enormous – granted, there is much to do! However, one of the great things about implementing VSO is that it's not something the developers have to do – there are tasks that others can help complete.

15

Leaving aside for a moment who does what, here's a list of some of the challenges we (as a unified team) will face:

- Adapting for Natural Language Processing (NLP) – Queries tend to be longer and more conversational, potentially using different phrasing for the same intent. It means we will need to accommodate this when working out the queries we want to support.

- Focusing on long-tail keywords – Unlike current searching, voice queries tend to be closer to questions rather than a mix of words strung together. Changing the make-up of queries will affect how our website ranks for specific, more natural-sounding phrases. We will need to answer questions that include terms such as "how" and "why" to align with search intent.

The aHrefs blog has a good article on implementing long-tail keywords and explaining why they will benefit your site. It is at `https://ahrefs.com/blog/long-tail-keywords/`.

- Making the site mobile-friendly – most voice searches occur on mobile devices, so sites need to be responsive, fast, and have a user-friendly interface for small screens.

- With more of an emphasis on making content more conversational, developers need to ensure this reflects in SEO – this affects anything from needing to implement structured data to making SEO more local and providing content easily picked up by SEO engines as if someone had asked a question.

- Along with making content more conversational, we must consider language and regional variations. A great example would be French – Parisians tend to speak a lot faster than, say, people from Alsace, plus the accent will be different (people from Alsace used to speak German, so there may well be a hint of it present). It's vital to ensure that voice recognition is accurate – it will not land well if the wrong content is given due to an incorrectly interpreted voice!

- We also need to not only make sure content is suitable for voice but also that the intent is understood and its context is relevant to its environment – for example, if we want "restaurants near me," to make sure they are indeed close, and not just a random selection.

- Accessibility will also be a challenge – not only do we need to adapt the interface to allow for voice commands, but we also need to make sure it works for people of lesser mobility, for example, if we make our site voice-accessible for a blind person, it will sink like a stone if screen-readers fail to read the site properly!

This is an interesting collection of thoughts to get us started – I'm sure there will be more, including those specific to your projects. One of the most essential points is keeping abreast of changes; implementing VSO isn't a one-off exercise but requires continuous maintenance, just as you would do with a car.

I suspect some stakeholders may think it's enough to implement one-time changes, but this will be a false economy; regional content might change, voice recognition is continually improving, and dialects alter over time. We may only need to do some of the work we'll cover later in the book as a one-off, but there will be tasks that we will need to revisit periodically to ensure we keep content fresh, accurate, and relevant for our customers. It's important to understand that implementing VSO is not a quick fix – it will take time and bring benefits gradually to the business.

Okay, I want to shift gears for a moment and touch on a topic I know is becoming more pertinent: artificial intelligence or AI.

Using AI: A Shift

What, may you ask, does AI have to do with voice search optimization?

It's a great question – as it so happens, AI can be helpful in several ways! It's not necessarily something we need to explore immediately, as we must focus on the basics first. However, there are a few areas we could explore, which might include these:

- We touched on the need to generate the right questions and the fact that understanding the intent is super-critical; AI can help confirm the context and purpose, making results more accurate and relevant for the user.

- AI is still relatively new but improving all of the time – there may be occasions where we might have to use complex queries, so it can help make better sense of interpreting and fulfilling those queries.

- AI is perfect for helping to identify areas where we can optimize our site: we will be able to deal with the obvious tasks like updating libraries, but AI could potentially help with refactoring the code base and removing redundant libraries or code. A good example might be swapping out an existing package for something more lightweight and up-to-date.

- We could use AI-driven analytics tools such as PaveAI (`https://www.paveai.com/`) to help better understand what people are searching for and help create content more relevant to our customers' needs.

- One of the most helpful ways we can use AI is to understand what customers are trying to say! Granted, this might sound a little controversial, but I'm referring to instances where a customer might have typed "apple" or "Apple." It's more likely that customers will have typed the former, but VSO won't necessarily know the difference: AI will understand the intent, correct the term, or search for content using the proper spelling.

Mmm, something worth thinking about! Implementing AI will be scary as it is so powerful, but we must remember that it is trained on vast amounts of data. If any of it is incomplete, it will start to hallucinate or provide inaccurate predictions based on the incomplete data.

The Your Digital Resource website at `https://www.yourdigitalresource.com/post/ai-for-voice-search-optimization` has a great article on how AI can play a role in optimizing for voice search; I've deliberately not included too many tools in this section to keep it as tool-agnostic as possible, but the article has some good examples you may like to consider when working on VSO.

Summary

Although standard search engine optimization has been around for a long time, VSO is still relatively new – it's not one single technology but a whole collection of processes and some new features. We've covered a lot of content around how to get started with it in this chapter, so let's take a moment to review what we learned.

We began with a quick introduction to voice search optimization (or VSO) before exploring how it works at a high level and why it differs from standard SEO. We then covered why it's essential to implement it in our sites before exploring some of the expectations around VSO and how it might present a few challenges for us to solve. To round out, we had a quick look at how AI can help support the implementation, from helping to optimize the site code to analyzing content and making suggestions around better phrases to use.

Okay, we've come to the end of the chapter: it's time to move on. I'm conscious that we've not covered anything practical yet from a developer perspective, but this is with good reason: we can't jump in until people are all up to speed!

In this chapter, we've made good progress. We still have some design considerations to work through, but we are getting closer to more practical matters! Without further ado, let's crack on and start to make some decisions about what we might need to change in the next chapter.

CHAPTER 2

Design Considerations

Up until now, we've learned about what VSO is, the benefits of implementing it, and the impact it will have on our site. However, there will come a point where someone mentions a particular word (or phrase containing that word). That word is **design**.

Yes, there are no two ways about it: VSO will not implement itself, and there will come a time when we have to start putting pen to paper, so to speak! VSO is still a relatively new topic, so there will be many questions to answer, even if some of it is based on existing practices. At this point, we'd typically come together and have one of those whiteboarding sessions. You know, the ones that either raise more questions than answers or send us down lots of rabbit holes … all to answer one question.

Where Do We Begin?

It's a great question – to answer, I'm reminded of something that someone I once knew said to me:

> *Forget the technology. Focus on what comes in, what needs to change, and what must come out at the end.*

It took a while for my somewhat naïve self (at the time!) to grasp what he meant, but there is a reason why: technology is just an enabler, a means to an end. You can always achieve what you want with it, but it's much better to look at what you need rather than how you do it to get the answer. If you can't do the former, then chances are, your plan isn't good and needs re-examining!

© Alex Libby 2025
A. Libby, *Beginning Voice Search Optimization*, Design Thinking,
https://doi.org/10.1007/979-8-8688-1841-7_2

It's why I would say the phrase describes VSO perfectly – as some of the steps (such as optimizing our site speed, dependencies, etc.) are already known, there will be a temptation to jump straight in and do this without really – **and I mean really** – understanding the bigger picture.

To help with this, we will work through some of the decisions we need to make when implementing VSO and understand who will be best to make those decisions or perform research if an answer isn't immediately available. Before we do this, though, there is one task we need to decide, which will block any future changes relating to VSO: are we using the best framework to run our site?

Assessing the Framework

Until now, we've concentrated on the theory behind VSO – looking at concepts such as what makes it beneficial to implement, its impact, and the challenges we might face.

One of the first challenges we must tackle is our choice of framework – does what we have suit our needs for VSO, or do we need to change? To understand where I'm coming from, let's consider an example.

Although I am focusing on React and Next.js here, the principles apply to frameworks like Vue or Angular.

Let's assume we're running a React-based site that's a few years old. It works well but could arguably do with a rewrite. We could stay with React, which would be a perfectly valid choice. Given we will need to make some potentially significant changes to both the UI and behind-the-scenes code (for the front end, not the back end) anyway, and that Next.js natively supports a number of the features we need to lean on, there may be a good argument for moving to Next.js.

It's important to note that React is a competent framework in its own right, and we can achieve everything we will cover in this book using this framework. However, if those features offered by Next.js extend and simplify the development process for implementing VSO, why not consider switching to using it? For example, if you use Sass in your setup, we would typically have to add this to the build process. This task isn't necessary with Next.js – support is already built in by default, so you can focus on writing the Sass code without worrying about the configuration! Using Sass is just one example of where Next.js differs – I've listed some more in Table 2-1.

Table 2-1. *Comparing React with Next.js*

Feature	Available in React?	Support in Next.js?
Server-side rendering (SSR)	Client-side-only built-in – SSR is possible with external tools such as ReactDOMServer	Next.js abstracts away complexities of SSR, making it easier to render server side with little help needed
Built-in CSS and Sass support	React doesn't provide built-in support for styling applications using CSS or Sass	Built-in by default, making it easy to integrate with other styling solutions
Static Site Generation (SSG)	Not included by default, but you can use tools like Gatsby. js to generate static sites from React components	Extends React to provide built-in support for static site generation
Automatic code splitting	Not included by default, but doable with tools such as Webpack	Integrated into Next.js, making for seamless splitting that loads bundles only when needed
Routing	Not built in by default – needs tools such as React Router to handle routing	It provides a file-based routing system, simplifying configuration and making it easier to manage in your application
API routes	React doesn't offer built-in support for creating API routes or serverless functions	Can create API routes as native serverless functions, making it seamless for fetching data or performing server-side operations in the application

23

From a developer perspective, though, there are a few reasons why we would want to consider moving to Next.js, in addition to what we covered in Table 2-1, which I've listed below:

- Network waterfalls, or when applications make sequential requests to fetch data, can cause performance issues – Next.js allows you to shift this to the server and choose in what order we build the UI, so pages build faster and layout shifting is reduced.

- We can choose how to fetch data – during build time, when requested, or on the client. It means that data could be cached to a CDN in some cases, making it faster to retrieve.

- Next.js already includes middleware by default, perfect for running code on the fly before a request is completed.

- Next.js has built-in components that can automatically optimize content such as media, fonts, or third-party scripts. This is especially important, given that VSO places a lot of emphasis on optimizing for speed (as would be the case for SEO, too) – anything we can do to optimize automatically will be a good thing!

There may still be some doubt as to whether you might want to make the change – to help with this, here are some questions you can answer:

- How old is your site? Is it using recent versions of React or built with versions from some years ago?

- Does your site use a lot of custom components that could be difficult to convert?

- Are you using lots of npm packages, and if so, how up-to-date are they? It shouldn't matter too much for Next.js, but this could throw up some unexpected issues with compatibility!

- Accessibility could be a factor: with current legislation, we need to ensure our site is as accessible as possible, so if we're under pressure, then spending time on a conversion may not be possible.

- Next.js can be used side by side with React, so it may be worth considering an upgrade/conversion for any subdomains you might be operating. We can, therefore, leave critical upgrades until the end, which will give you time to allow Next.js to bed in and surface any issues that need addressing before we tackle the more critical areas of the site.

Of course, you may decide that Next.js isn't for you and that React is the way forward – this is equally fine, but you will be missing out on features that will make development more straightforward for you.

If you decide to change the framework and go for something like Next.js, then it's also worth checking what hosting you want to use. Our hosting choice can also impact speed (and ultimately SEO) – I'll return to this later in this chapter.

Okay, let's move on: now we've covered the benefits of implementing VSO at a high level and explored some of the reasons why Next.js may be a preferable option; let's switch gears and take a look at some of the areas we need to focus on when it comes to implementing VSO. We'll begin with assembling the team.

Assembling the Team

Cast your mind back to earlier – do you remember that I said that implementing VSO requires a team of people from across several functions?

From experience, I've seen instances where developers are not (at least immediately) involved in any changes being discussed in conversations between Product Owners and UX designers. While this is probably accepted practice, it means that, as developers, we miss out on understanding why certain decisions have been made and can't challenge any issues we see until after designs have been signed off. Clearly not an ideal place to be!

Getting everyone together is one of those occasions where it will be particularly beneficial, even for the initial process of working out who will do which task. Everyone knows who is involved, we can have open and honest discussions, and hopefully, we can go away with at least the initial ideas that UX can turn into a formal design. As developers, it will also allow us to establish what changes we might need to make to existing processes – do not forget that traditional SEO and VSO have similar optimization requirements, so we don't want to reinvent the wheel for the latter!

For this book, I'm going to assume that we're starting from scratch – at a high level, there are four main areas where people will be required, which I've listed in Table 2-2.

Table 2-2. *Roles required in developing VSO*

Task	Owner/Team	At a High Level
Providing content, researching existing analytics metrics, and determining what needs changing/updating	Analytics	Need to provide long-tail queries and content optimized for speech
Updating the framework in use, plus implementing the code changes required	Architecture and developers	Decide if the existing framework is the right one or if it needs to be updated/changed
Creating and/or updating the UI designs	UX designers	Update the website designs, media, and assets
Determining privacy changes and impacts	Security/business	VSO will create concerns around data privacy and GDPR – these need to be assessed, and any changes implemented to address/ mitigate concerns
Promoting changes throughout the business and to customers	Product owners and associated stakeholders	Making sure people are aware of upcoming changes, enabling support, and increasing awareness

As you can see from the table, there is scope for everyone to take part – a lot of this will depend on who performs the role in your company, but it's a perfect excuse to help promote cross-team or departmental collaboration, which will be a good thing!

Okay, let's move on – we've talked about exploring whether the existing framework needs to be updated and what roles everyone will play; it's time now for us to break down what we need to do into more clearly defined tasks. We'll take a look at what I call "non-developer" tasks momentarily, but let's first begin with the more technical needs.

Breaking Down the Developer Tasks

When it comes to implementing VSO, collaboration will be critical to the whole process – we have a range of tasks to work through, some of which will require outside support.

Do not forget that we don't have to do all of them in one go – indeed, it will be better to phase in changes so that we can assess the impact and pivot if required in the future. Let's take a high-level look at them in turn before exploring them in more detail later in this book:

- Assess the framework – this is something we've already touched on, but it will be crucial to everything we do: should we rebuild using something like Next.js instead of staying with React?

- This next point is crucial – we must be mindful of the scope of change and work out who does what, when, and how – oh, and why! It goes without saying that this book aims to help with that process, but I can't stress enough that we need to be on top of scope throughout! VSO is a significant change that will be new for everyone, so keeping the scope in check will help minimize the impact on the business.

- Minimize HTTP requests: A part of SEO (and, by extension, VSO) is the need for speed – one way we can do this is by reducing or combining the number of elements (images, scripts, stylesheets) on each page to minimize HTTP requests. We, as developers, should be doing this as a matter of course, but VSO will accentuate the need for a fast site.

- A developer task we need to explore is enabling browser caching – this allows visitors' browsers to store certain elements of our website temporarily, reducing the need to download resources again and resulting in faster load times.

- In the same vein, we should look at optimizing images, particularly to reduce the size of any that are large, which can significantly slow down our website. As long as we do this with care, it won't compromise the quality but will help reduce file size and improve loading speed. As developers, our build process should be doing this automatically, but we must include any we add as part of implementing VSO.

- Optimize for mobile – in today's world, this is a no-brainer: more people look at websites from mobile devices than standard desktop machines. By default, we should be using the mobile-first approach when developing if we don't already – if not, then now might be a good time to consider a rebuild first!

- VSO emphasizes the need to use a reliable service provider, particularly one that uses content delivery networks (CDNs), to help distribute our website's static files across multiple servers worldwide. Both will affect website speed – customers can access content quicker as we cache resources nearer their physical location (American customers use US-based servers, Irish use European, etc.). Your site may be using CDNs already, in which case this isn't an issue – if not, then it's worth exploring options, depending on which hosting provider you use (or plan to use).

- We've already touched on the need to reduce the number of resources we use – at the same time, we should also make sure we minify resources where possible. The obvious candidates are CSS and JavaScript, but I tend to shy away from minifying HTML, as it can make debugging difficult. (I will leave it up to you to decide if you include HTML in this process!)

- We need to look at the keywords used in the search process. Typically, these will be short phrases or select words, but VSO encourages using long-tail keywords or ones that resemble questions rather than simple phrases. In conjunction with using long-tail keywords, we also need to switch to using more conversational language in our content.

- Prioritizing local SEO is also something we as a business need to look at – ensuring we've updated search engines with content such as business names, images, and addresses. We'll explore this more later in the book, but for now, think of this as entering a search term such as "restaurants near me" and then clicking on one of the results returned by the search engine you use.

- Try to capture Google featured snippets – this is something that may be technically easy to set up but can be complicated to get right: it requires careful research into the types of keywords we want to use, it takes time to refine the content, and there is no guarantee Google will use our results as featured snippets.

- Use schema markup – although this is possible if using React, Next.js makes it easier to implement using the built-in metadata option. We can't do it so easily with standard React, as we need to use a third-party plugin such as react-helmet. It's not impossible, but it's yet another dependency we could well do without!

- Speech recognition – this makes VSO work; it will open up a real can of worms if we're not careful, and one where we could end up going down a massive proverbial rabbit warren! It will tie in with the work we need to do to add support for Natural Language Processing (NLP), plus adapting analytics to support voice.

As it's a large part of what we must do, we'll look at this in more detail in Chapter 4.

- We need to build processes to keep everything up to date, including algorithms, trends, keywords, tags, and content. This step could present a challenge, though, as I know from experience that time pressures are such that many teams do not have time or the resources to do this very often! It's mainly down to prioritization – for other projects of this nature, only those that bring in revenue will go to the top of the list. The irony here is that while VSO may not directly affect revenue, minor changes, and tweaks will impact revenue – it means that we need to build in time and resources to keep on top of any changes we need to implement once VSO is in place.

Phew – there's plenty for us to do: we only scratch the surface on some topics, such as adding speech recognition capabilities, making changes to the UI, or even looking after anyone visiting from different countries!

Before we get into the specifics around making these changes, there are two topics I want to cover from the get-go – dealing with UX and stakeholders. This process *can* be tricky if we're not careful – let's look at what we need to consider in more detail.

Designing the UX Experience

I mentioned earlier that implementing VSO is not limited to developer-led changes – we have changes that need to be looked at by others, too! We briefly saw earlier the kind of changes that others outside of the developer team need to work on – let's take a look at the first of those for the UX team.

We can complete many of these changes in parallel with those done by others outside of the developer team – planning this will be a real test, but worth it!

- We must be mindful of how we expect customers to use our interface: Is it for purchasing items, asking questions, or something else?

- As part of designing the UI, UX should consider what extra media are needed and where UI differences might exist, such as mobile devices having built-in microphones but tablets not. How will this affect the overall experience for customers? We would need icons for those features, to show the state (enabled or disabled), but how can we effectively block the icons from being downloaded if a device doesn't support that feature? Icons might be tiny in size, but if we're using a lot of them, this will have a cumulative effect over time, where we're downloading unnecessary media which makes the site run slower.

- Although much of what we will look at in this book will be for VSO, we should remember that our changes will likely benefit those with disabilities. We obviously can't cater to everyone, but is there a way to ascertain if any of our customers have physical needs that VSO could help, at least indirectly? It's important to consider what would be acceptable to ask customers so (a) we're not discriminatory and (b) we cater to where we can have the most impact.

- Feedback is another area UX will need to consider: what would the happy path be for customers, and how should we (i.e., the company) handle any instances where customers fall off this happy path? (This will be part of the development process, but I'm thinking more about the user experience at this stage!)

- In terms of prioritization, how much do we want to include in terms of changes, and what order? There will be things that the UX team can do, such as work out what changes we would need if we were to implement all of the changes and highlight any issues that might pop up, which could affect how much we can implement. Ultimately, though, we will need to have conversations with stakeholders to ascertain the overall plan – I'll come back to this later in this chapter.

Phew – I've covered a lot of points here: probably too many! The reality is that VSO will require a lot of changes; it is still relatively new, but it will be worth the changes, provided we have a solid plan in place and build-in time to refine changes as we progress through the implementation.

Considering Accessibility

This next batch of tasks is one we, as developers, would need to share with the UX designers – they all relate to accessibility.

If you've done anything with accessibility, you will know it is potentially a massive topic: probably one worthy of a book in its own right. However, this is one area that is super critical to complete – there is an increasing legal requirement to ensure sites are accessible where possible.

The great thing about implementing accessibility changes is that the improvements we need to make (such as better semantics, cleaner structure, and so on) help provide better cues for search engines to implement and deliver more relevant content. If we can integrate both strategies, we will cater to a broader audience while keeping a user-friendly experience for everyone who visits the site.

Keeping this in mind, let's run through the kind of tasks we'll need to look at for our site in more detail – these will likely be ones that both developers and UX designers need to work through:

- Design clear and accessible voice search triggers, such as microphone icons, that encourage users to engage with voice search features.

- Provide visual or auditory feedback when visitors initiate a voice search so we can confirm to users that we are processing their query.

- Display voice search results in an easily digestible format, allowing users to find the information they need quickly.

- Build in a process to review any changes made regularly, as voice search technology is still improving and will likely affect what we put into place now and in the future.

- Make sure any changes to the UI still conform with the agreed business branding, including colors. Customers never really like change, so it's essential that everything follows a cohesive design and that new elements do not stick out and scare customers!

- Perform extensive research with selected customers – use the opportunity to elaborate on what the business wants to implement and work through specific design aspects. Customers may not like speaking to their computers (at least initially), but given time and a bit of handholding, they will get used to it! Early inclusion means that for any mockups you create, you can ask customers which they prefer; it will help us increase engagement and reduce uncertainty when implementing the UI for VSO.

I'm sure there will be more – as I've mentioned before, it's probably more important to make this a collaborative exercise so that teams can work through any challenges as they appear. Talking of challenges, it's important to note that accessibility isn't immune; some gotchas might trip us up if we're not careful! Let's take a look at a few in more detail so you get a flavor of what to expect – I've listed some in Table 2-3.

Table 2-3. *Challenges with VSO and accessibility*

	Challenge	Solution
Content Presentation Conflicts	Voice search often relies on concise answers, but accessibility standards recommend providing detailed, well-structured information for screen readers and users with cognitive impairments	Balance brevity for voice search and depth for accessibility. Use "expandable content" (e.g., FAQ accordions) to offer concise answers upfront while allowing for more detailed explanations
Complex or Missing Navigation	Poorly designed navigation can confuse voice search algorithms and make your site inaccessible to screen readers	Create simple, logical navigation structures with descriptive link text and accessible menu designs. Ensure ARIA (Accessible Rich Internet Applications) roles are implemented properly
Media Content Without Alternatives	Multimedia content (like videos or podcasts) optimized for voice search may not include captions, transcripts, or alternative descriptions, hindering accessibility	Provide transcripts for audio/video content and add captions to videos to ensure both accessibility and voice search compatibility
Structured Data Misalignment	Using schema markup to optimize voice search can sometimes exclude accessibility metadata (e.g., descriptions for screen readers)	Use comprehensive schema markup with accessible metadata, such as `imageAlt,` for visual content and accessible content labels
Dynamic Content Challenges	Voice search favors dynamic content updates, but such content may not always be accessible (e.g., live chat, auto-updating feeds)	Ensure dynamic content is accessible by using ARIA live regions and testing with assistive technologies

This checklist is just a start – hopefully, it's enough to get conversations flowing and an early plan formed! I am sure there will be other questions to ask, but many will come later. The essential point here is that people see this as an ongoing process so developers can turn UX designs into reality while maintaining accessibility as much as possible throughout the site.

Okay, we have two more teams to talk to: both are just as important and probably the real test of whether we are successful! I'm referring to Analytics as proof of whether the results we get back are good, and finally stakeholders – have we done everything we can, and does it all work? Let's look at both, beginning with how Analytics will play a role in implementing VSO.

Working with Analytics

So far, we've talked about the things we'll need to change when implementing VSO; however, we'll need to know if our changes have the desired effect.

To do this, we will need to update the analytics on our site and ensure that we're monitoring the right actions. Although this work is primarily for the Analytics team, some collaboration will be required with developers and Product Owners to ensure all tags are covered and that we get the right results coming through in the Analytics tools.

With all of that in mind, there are three main areas we need to focus on – this may not seem as complex as the work that the developers will do, but each area will still have a fair few changes to make:

- The biggest challenge will be creating long-tail keywords, based around 3-4 words in a longer phrase – voice recognition works best when using Natural Language Processing (NLP). In other words, the content needs to be something we could ask as a question. A lot of this will be based on what people are asking now, but given this will be a different style of content to what is in use, the Analytics team will need to create a transition strategy from existing keywords and actions to ones based more around NLP.

- The next challenge will be updating the tags against elements on the page, such as adding tags for speech icons/buttons or customer feedback. Once the Analytics team agrees on which tags we should add, and developers have done so, they can ensure results come through correctly – this can form the basis of a transition plan to either move from simple queries to more NLP-based questions or adapt the results to include both.

- We've talked about needing to transition to new tags, but there is one thing we need to consider – given we have new tags in place, plus new content for VSO, we need to agree on how to manage the transition in the analytics results that come back. There will be a transitionary period where results start to include NLP queries; we need to agree on this with the business and other stakeholders so everyone knows the changes and how this might influence upcoming business decisions.

This should be enough to get the Analytics team started – I would recommend attacking this work in stages and potentially leaving a period between each stage to allow metrics to start filtering through. I think the key for all of this is to have a concrete plan in place – it may require some discussions with the Product Owner and stakeholders to ensure they know that there will be changes coming and that we will have to phase them in over time!

Okay, let's crack on. We have one more task, which is probably one of the most important – talking to stakeholders! This is where we may have to tread carefully, depending on our relationship; setting reasonable expectations will be key to success. Let's dive in and take a look at this in more detail.

Engaging with Stakeholders

This stage is probably the most challenging part of implementing change, as some will want a design that looks great but raises all manner of issues when turning it into reality!

While many will be supportive of what we do, there will be some who can be – shall we say – a little inflexible and may not understand why something they ask us to do isn't possible when they expect it to be done exactly the way they want it …. It kind of reminds me of something I saw on a LinkedIn post:

> *They needed more people who understood the product and knew what to build first.*

Think about this for a moment: What usually happens in a typical development process? As developers, we typically only see the designs once they have been completed and signed off, right? We work through them, decide what tasks need doing, and work out sprint points … you get the idea.

While this process usually works, there is a downside to it. If any of my experience is to go by, we almost always find an issue with the design that requires further development or refactoring, resulting in a delay before we can get started. A perfect example is the use of icons – while UX might create something flashy that stakeholders love, the resulting file size will likely cause us problems, and we must change the design to something smaller and lighter! Sound familiar? We frequently end up with a back-and-forth between us developers, the Product Owner, and the stakeholders – it gets frustrating, blocks anything we can do, and so on.

I know that the typical process is for product owners to work on designs with stakeholders and then filter down the results to developers once they have approved them. However, implementing VSO is one of those occasions where I strongly believe it will pay developers to collaborate with stakeholders and Product Owners during the design process and not just be responsible for writing code at the end. Let me explain why.

As we will see throughout this book, some of the changes we need to make will be ones that we would have to do anyway, such as optimizing CSS files, so we only use the rules required for our site. The flip side of this is that there will be some features we need to implement that will be new to developers, stakeholders, UX, and those looking after SEO. To get around this, there are a few things we can do (not necessarily in any particular order):

- Build some demos that show the basics of those features that are new, such as voice recognition.

- Invite stakeholders into a workshop where we can run these demos: make it clear that this is to show off what is possible and that the demos are there to help crystalize requirements into something solid to which people can relate.

- Work through the changes suggested in this book and split them into groups – those developers can handle (as part of normal business activities) and those requiring further discussions with stakeholders. We can remove the need to involve stakeholders in tasks that will be internal to the developer team; stakeholders need to appreciate the importance of doing them and not just focus on the shiny new toys!

- Assemble some guidelines around requirements such as the natural language queries: work on the basis that we're illustrating the phrasing we could use, but it's up to others to finalize what we should use on the site.

- As part of demoing any proof-of-concept examples, we must emphasize what it means for the customer and indicate how long it might take to implement some of the newer features. I know not all of this will be possible upfront, but the intention here is to try to be open and set some expectations around complexity. After all, we don't want to rush through anything that ends up breaking the site if we're not aligned from the outset! At the same time, it may be better to understand everything we need to change, but we should do it in phases if demands on time and resources make it impossible to implement in one big project.

I'm sure there will be more we can do to help with stakeholder engagement as we work through the book – VSO is still relatively new as a topic, so collaboration will play a crucial part in implementing this technology in your projects.

What About the Future?

We've almost reached the end of this chapter and are nearly at the point where we start creating changes to our site. Before we do so, I want to ask a question: what about the future?

Indeed, I've already mentioned that implementing VSO is one of those topics that really needs ongoing maintenance, much like traditional SEO. However, this raises a question as to what we can do to develop our installation once VSO is in place – here are a few ideas as a starting point:

- VSO offers increased accuracy and personalization: we've already touched on how it should return a more concise, accurate set of results than we might get now. As NLP matures, we can expect these results to become even smaller and more focused on that user's preferences, search history, and context.

- On personalization, it's worth considering the impact on A/B testing (or experimentation) – how would VSO affect it? If the results returned are highly focused, personalization will be even more helpful, as the most popular choice for customers will better reflect reality.

- This next topic might seem a little "out there" – what devices could we use for searching? Smart speakers and cell phones are the devices that most people use, but imagine if we could search from a wearable piece of technology, using, say, a kit such as a Raspberry Pico? It might seem a little far-fetched, but the technology is essentially already here – it will just take someone to figure out how to connect the dots.

- One of the more important concepts to think about is voice commerce. Imagine using a microphone (of some description) to talk to a website and trigger a purchase! It would work particularly well with Google or Apple Pay or potentially the Payment Request API already in the browser – we just need to link this to VSO to get that end-to-end solution.

- The last one I want to cover is the scope and use of AI: could this help refine searches or suggest better options based on what people have asked, for example?

It may well trigger data privacy concerns, but they are
not insurmountable; it will take time for people to get
used to it and for us to build controls so people feel safe
about using the site.

Mmm, there are some interesting ideas there, for sure! The great thing
is that we're still in the relatively early days of VSO (and AI, for that matter),
so there is plenty of opportunity to find out what is possible and see
whether it works for us. Granted, it may scare people, but this is why we
have development environments – we need to build in time to experiment
a little to see if something works for us and whether it will help improve
what we already have in our environment.

Summary

Implementing VSO can potentially be a real rabbit warren – there is so
much we can do, and it links to lots of different technologies, so it's very
easy for us to get led into avenues that end up with no result! In a way,
this doesn't matter – VSO is still new so there will be things we need to
investigate, and as they say, you don't know until you try! With that in
mind, we've covered some interesting points in this chapter, so let's take a
moment to review what we have learned.

We started by asking that perennial question, "Where do we begin?"
(that seems so apt, yet corny too!), before addressing the topic of
assessing whether we want to stay with our current framework or switch
to something like Next.js. At the same time, we detailed the various teams
that should be involved, as a minimum – others may need to come in, but
the list should provide a starting point for any work we do.

Next, we broke down the task areas for the developers, before
considering what they may also need to look at in terms of UX,
accessibility, and analytics. To round out, we then covered the thorny
question of engaging with stakeholders – I say thorny as we may not know

how they take the changes: some could be all for it, while others may (understandably) be less enthusiastic! We will only know when we broach the subject with them, so hopefully, some of the comments in this chapter will help ease future conversations.

Okay – let's move on: we've spent a lot of time reviewing theory and various discussion points, but it's time we got stuck into more coding matters. I know what we've covered might seem like a lot, but VSO is a weighty topic that can impact our site if we don't get it right! Thankfully, we've done the hard, theoretical work, so it's all code from here on. We've got a lot to cover, so we'll start with the site optimization work – stay with me, and I'll take you through everything in the next chapter.

CHAPTER 3

Optimizing Content

Until now, we've talked about what voice search optimization is and explored some of the design factors we need to consider when implementing VSO – it's time to put pen to paper (at least metaphorically speaking) and commit to changes!

Over the following few pages, we will look at optimizing content – while our copy needs to be good, the reality is that it isn't just content but also areas of the code base that we need to make sure are optimized, too. This optimizing process could open a real can of worms, depending on how well-maintained your site is (or – heaven forbid – not), so before we begin updating code, let's first set a few assumptions about how we will manage the optimization process.

Setting Some Assumptions

Cast your mind back to Chapter 2, particularly the section "Breaking Down the Developer Tasks." You will note that many tasks fall into the optimization bucket, such as making sure images are in the best format, browser caching, mobile design, and minimizing resource usage, to name a few.

Optimizing plays a crucial role in implementing VSO – Google has been very coy about exactly what it looks for when it comes to VSO, but it's a sure bet that a site that hasn't been optimized won't do it any favors! With

© Alex Libby 2025
A. Libby, *Beginning Voice Search Optimization*, Design Thinking,
https://doi.org/10.1007/979-8-8688-1841-7_3

that thought in mind and to help guide us through this chapter, I'm going to make a few assumptions:

- I will refer to either voice or smart assistant interchangeably: please assume I'm referring to the same thing unless I say otherwise in the text. The critical point here is that no matter the name, I'm referring to a device we can control by voice and interface with the Web.

- We'll continue to base much of this content on React and Next.js, but please do not let this prevent you from implementing VSO. We could equally apply similar techniques across different frameworks – the key here is more about understanding the principles of what we need to do, not the specifics of how to do it for our chosen framework.

For this book, I will use two sites. One will be the Apress website, which we will only use to illustrate issues. The second will be a smaller demo site I've created, where we can make the necessary changes.

- I'm assuming your usual daily work is as part of a wider team where you have a product owner, UX designers who will have a say in these changes, and stakeholders who will see the impact of these changes once the new features are in place. If this is not the case, please refine as needed – it's more important to understand what is required and that someone can take care of a task where needed.

- Although I've aimed this book primarily at developers, we should not forget that implementing VSO is a collaborative process. We need to include anyone responsible for the main direction of the website (typically a Product Owner), individuals who look after SEO generally, plus anyone who deals with hosting (depending on what you use).

Excellent – now we have that out of the way, let's start with the next task: preparing a demo site to help with understanding and performing optimization.

Preparing Our Site

For this chapter, I've created a demo site, which I will call "Alexander Libby Ceramics" – you can see the code in the download accompanying this book. Let's get it up and running.

LAUNCHING THE DEMO SITE

To get the demo running, first make sure you have Node.js installed on your platform (which you will likely have anyway), then follow these steps:

1. First, go ahead and extract a copy of the demo-site folder from the code download accompanying this book – save it to your C: drive (or chosen location).

2. Crack open a Node.js terminal session, then change the working folder to the demo-site folder in Step 1.

3. At the prompt, enter npm run dev and hit Enter – you should then be able to browse to the site, which is hosted at http://localhost:3000/ . If all is well, you should see something similar to the extract shown in Figure 3-1.

47

Figure 3-1. *Extract of demo site for the optimization work*

When you explore the demo, you will notice I've kept it simple for a reason. It's at times like this that I'm reminded of a particular proverb:

Give a man a fish, and you feed him for a day. Teach him how to fish, and you feed him for a lifetime.

This is one of those occasions where I *could* give you a set of tools to optimize your site, but there's a risk that these tools may not work for every site you work on. If you happen to work on both, say, React and Angular sites, then it clearly won't work on the latter!

The better thing to do is understand where to make changes – a great example is images. You should be doing it anyway, but if this isn't the case, we need to make sure image sizes are as small as possible. It's at this point where you need to ask yourself questions such as these (in no particular order):

1.   Do you have an optimization process in place that uses something like a npm or PostCSS package? If so, is it optimized to the best it can be, or does it need adjusting?

2. What image format(s) do you use – is it standard
    PNG, and could a format like WebP (or even SVG),
    work better for you?

3. Which images are really large and could do with
    going on a diet?

4. What would you classify as being a candidate for
    optimization – anything over 20KB, for example?

5. Are there any images that you no longer need and
    could do with removing?

See what I mean? We can start by understanding where we need changes,
but it will be down to you to understand how to change based on what you
have in your code environment and what works best for your needs.

Okay, let's crack on: before we get into assessing how well our site is
optimized, there is something important I want to cover, which is some of
the challenges we face with SEO when using frameworks such as React,
upon which Next.js is built. There are a couple of things we need to note,
so let's take a look at them in more detail.

The Challenges of SEO and React

One of the challenges we face when using React for SEO is that React relies
on client-side rendering – this makes content less accessible to the likes
of Google and Bing when compared to plain HTML. It isn't ideal, as it
can make indexing slower and negatively affect rankings – not something
we want! It will be even worse if the site is slow, impacting both the user
experience and SEO. Can we do anything about this?

In short, yes, we can, but it will depend on which version of Next.js you
use – hopefully, this will be a recent edition (ideally version 15); older versions
are still acceptable but require more work and extra plugins. If you decided
to go with vanilla React, this is still possible but will likely require even

49

more work to set up, as much of what helps Next.js to offer that improved experience will already be baked in or more straightforward to set up!

Leaving aside which version of Next.js you use (and I'm assuming it's version 15 for this chapter), there are some checks and tasks we can perform to help improve the setup for SEO:

- Enable Server-Side Rendering (SSR) – SSR renders HTML on the server, which improves load times and enables search engines to index content better. In Next.js 15, a lot of this is built-in; if needed, you can use plugins like React Helmet, Gatsby Image, and React Router to help enhance SEO.

- Implement meaningful URLs and metadata – we need to use descriptive URLs, titles, and metadata to help search engines better understand and rank our content.

- Optimizing media – compressing images, using proper formats, and optimizing alt tags and captions will help improve page speed and user experience.

We can still achieve similar improvements in older versions of Next.js but need to use a plugin such as the React-Helmet one I mentioned just now, which is available from `https://www.npmjs.com/package/react-helmet`. It's worth noting that Next.js has its own `<Head>` component for this purpose, but React-Helmet offers much more advanced functionality, such as managing tags across different components.

If you would like to see more about how we can use react-helmet in a Next.js application, take a look at the article on the Medium website by Farihatul Maria at `https://medium.com/@farihatulmaria/enhancing-seo-in-next-js-with-react-helmet-integration-386af0c067c9`.

Okay, let's move on: We've seen some of the challenges that affect us when it comes to SEO in Next.js and how we can get around them; what does this mean for VSO? Interestingly, it's more of the same, but with some changes to allow for voice – let's take a look.

What Affects Voice SEO?

Cast your mind back to Chapter 1 – if you can – and you will hopefully remember that I alluded to the fact that VSO isn't a single technology but a list of tasks we must work through to implement it. It means a host of changes, all of which need prioritizing; some of these you will hopefully already be doing, but VSO will help increase their priority. The list falls into roughly five different areas:

- Updating the framework used

- Optimizing the site

- Providing optimized content

- Creating and/or refining search queries (that use natural language)

- Creating and/or updating the UI

We've already talked about the first one, namely, the framework we're using – we covered that Next.js offers some useful features that make it easier to implement SEO (and, by default, VSO). Though the big elephant in the room is optimizing, the details we will be exploring momentarily, the remaining two are specific to VSO and relate to how customers will see and use our search facilities.

Okay, enough of the theory: it's time for us to get stuck into optimizing! Optimization is a vast topic and one we can't do complete justice to in this book, as I'm sure you're aware. However, there are some tasks we can do to help get us at least part way there – we'll go through all of them later in this chapter, but the first one involves using a very familiar tool.

Testing with Lighthouse

"Ladies and gentlemen – it's time..." Indeed, it is time – time to test our sites!

One of the best ways to assess (and optimize) our site is already built into the browser – I'm talking about Chrome's Lighthouse tool. In case you've not already used it, it runs a series of audits against any chosen page and generates a report based on what it finds and recommends should be fixed (for mobile and desktop).

It covers a range of topics, but I'm particularly interested in SEO and Accessibility – to see what it comes up with, we'll test the Apress homepage and our demo site, before exploring what changes we might need to make in more detail.

ASSESSING LIGHTHOUSE: EXAMPLE

For this next demo, I will use two sites as an example – our test demo site that we set up at the start of this chapter, plus Apress's site. I know we can't fix the issues on that one(!), but it's still good to see what – if anything – is revealed when we run our tests.

Before we get stuck in, we need to set a few assumptions to ensure a level playing field throughout the tests; these are all set before we run the tests:

- I'm closing any cookie banners that appear (such as on Apress's site).

- We will run all tests in an incognito browser: there is something to be said for potentially running them with pages already open in a browser so you can see how the site performs in a real-world scenario. I haven't seen any official guidance on what is best, so either will work – the key is ensuring consistency across all of your tests.

- All tests are being run in current versions of Chrome, as Lighthouse is already enabled by default.

- This demo will focus on SEO and Performance; Accessibility will come later in the chapter.

- You will see that I'm running checks on Apress's website at `https://www.apress.com`, but it redirects to include a two-letter code at the end. Don't worry – this is expected: it will redirect you to a version that reflects your location. The same principles apply, irrespective of which country version your browser renders on screen.

Note that you will likely get different results if running in separate browsers on different machines; it all depends on the available resources, which will impact testing. I would run the tests in a CI pipeline rather than directly on a PC or Mac to ensure consistency.

With this in mind, let's begin the demo – I'm using a PC, but if you are using a Mac, please use the Cmd button anytime you see a reference to the Ctrl button:

1. First, fire up your browser and head to Apress's main website, at `https://www.apress.com`.

2. Press F12 or Ctrl+Shift+I to bring up the Developer Console, and click the Lighthouse tab.

3. Hit the Desktop option under Device, then click Analyze page load to the right. Wait for it to complete the test.

4. When the test is complete, you will see something akin to the result shown in Figure 3-2.

Figure 3-2. *Results of the Lighthouse test for the Apress site (Desktop)*

5. Next, fire up a Node.js terminal session, then change the working folder to the demo site we created at the start of this chapter.

6. At the prompt, enter npm run dev and press Enter – this will start the Next.js development server.

7. Repeat steps two to four to get the results for the demo site in Desktop conditions.

8. If all is well, you should see something akin to those shown in Figure 3-3.

Figure 3-3. *Results of the Lighthouse test for the demo site (Desktop)*

Ouch! There are some differences there – not to put too fine a point on it, but there is work to do! Don't worry, though – it's not all as bad as it looks; before we get too worried about the finer details, there are some key points to note, so let's dive in and take a look at them in more detail.

Understanding the Changes Made

One of the best ways I've seen to audit sites is to use Google's Lighthouse applet – it focuses on four main areas: Performance, Accessibility, SEO, and Best Practices. We ran the Lighthouse audit for both the Apress and localhost sites in Desktop mode – Mobile will come momentarily. In each case, all the results are laid out for us to view, along with links and tips to help improve any areas that fall short of the 100% mark.

Although Lighthouse is great at auditing, there are a couple of niggles that can get in the way – I touched on some of them before we ran the test:

- We can only test on a per-page basis if we're using the applet in the browser; we need to repeat the audit process for every page, which isn't always feasible.

- I can guarantee that if you run the tests multiple times on the same page and in the same browser, you will see different results appear on most tests! Lighthouse's audit process depends on available resources on the machine you run the tests; if the host machine is busy, tests will be slower, and results may not be as high as they should be.

Even though there are some limitations, the tests identified several areas where we need to make improvements. I know we won't be able to do so for the Apress site, but looking at the flagged issues is still a worthwhile cause, as you may see the same issue appear on your sites.

Reviewing the Results: What Do We Need to Improve?

So, what results did we get back? When I ran the tests on my PC, I noticed issues in all four areas, with Performance worst at 51% and Accessibility the highest at 86%. We'll look at Accessibility later in this chapter, but let's focus first on Performance, followed by SEO.

We would still need to improve the Best Practices section, too, so it hits as close to 100% as possible – it's not the main focus of what we're looking at right now, though!

Performance Issues for Apress

So, for the Apress site, I noted a lot of performance issues for Desktop, some of which I've listed below:

- Images need resizing/displaying in next-gen formats.

- Adding width and height to images.

- JavaScript on the site needs to be slimmed down: third-party scripts are affecting speed, and Lighthouse flagged a lot of unused scripts. The site also seems to have some legacy JavaScript, which would be a prime candidate for audit and potential removal!

- Defer offscreen images.

- Caching seems to be an issue.

- DOM is huge at 659 elements – this needs attention.

I must admit that it was a little scary seeing all those issues flagged when looking at the report! They vary from red (critical) to white (less critical or just information only). It highlights the benefits of iterating through the issues; it's not a matter of who did what or why, but drawing a line underneath and fixing the issue so we have a good baseline to work against in implementing VSO.

SEO Issues for Apress

The results of this test turned out to be a lot easier for the SEO section – Lighthouse only identified two issues compared to the more extensive list for Performance!

Digging into the results, I found the following flagged as issues that would need resolving:

- Links not crawlable

- No valid `hreflang` attribute

Let's assume you see similar issues on your site – if we had to fix them, I'd want to first look at where they are coming from. Fortunately, Lighthouse provides a list of where it has identified the issues, and in this case, the issues are coming from links used in the footer.

The issue is that several links use the `<a>` tag, but Lighthouse has noticed that the href element is missing. We have a couple of options open to us: we could mark these as non-crawlable in the `robots.txt` file, use a different element that doesn't need the `href` tag, or we can add that `href` tag in if we deem them to be eligible for crawling.

For the `hreflang` issue, this is potentially a little easier to solve – it looks like the issues are coming from these links (an example of which I've highlighted in Figure 3-4.

```
ᵗˢ, ᵗᵗᵒˢˢˢᵗᵉᵒ⁷ᵗˢˢˢᵒ ⁷
<link rel="alternate" href="/cn" hreflang="zh-CN"> == $0
<link rel="alternate" href="/kr" hreflang="ko-KR">
<link rel="alternate" href="/jp" hreflang="ja">
<link rel="alternate" href="/br" hreflang="pt-BR">
```

Figure 3-4. *One of the links flagged for an invalid hreflang tag*

I did some digging for this issue – it seems that Lighthouse is flagging that the `hreflang` tags appear not to be valid, as they need to be two-digit codes, and not as we have in this example. The `hreflang` refers to the *spoken* language (in this case, Chinese), not that it's being spoken in China – it's one of those issues we just need to fix. It might be possible to pull this kind of information dynamically but to be honest, it'll be simpler just to add the code as it stands!

Okay, we've seen some of the issues that could appear on the Apress site; let's switch sites and look at the demo site we set up earlier. This time, though, we can go one step further and implement some of the fixes – let's dive in and take a look at what Lighthouse has in store for us.

Performance Issues for the Demo Site

Having just done the checks on the Apress site, I wasn't sure what to expect this time for the demo site – would it show similar issues or something completely different? Well, it turns out that there were some similarities, at least where JavaScript was concerned! Let's have a look at some of what I found:

- The above fold image is lazily loaded, which can slow performance as it is not loaded immediately.

- Lighthouse alerted that JavaScript used in the site needs to be minified, and an audit is done to reduce unused scripts.

- Lighthouse flagged that some legacy JavaScript is being served and that we should check to see if we can reduce or remove any of it.

- Some of the payloads were too large, so we need to look at Next.js's configuration to see if we can reduce payload sizes.

- Lighthouse identified some page caching issues.

None of these should be show stoppers – as before, we should take this as an opportunity to fix the issues listed (or update code to design them out) so that we have a clean base ready to continue implementing VSO.

SEO Issues for the Demo Site

When I ran the Lighthouse audit on the demo site, it flagged a couple of issues we need to address – they are probably the most straightforward changes we will need to make! They are

- The site is missing a `title` tag.

- The site doesn't have a `meta` tag or description present.

To fix both issues only requires a small change to one file – it's almost not worth an exercise in its own right! Crack open the `page.js` file at the root of your project (in `\src\app`), then add this block after the last `import` statement:

```
export const metadata = {
  title: "Demo Site for Optimization",
  description: "This is a demo site for optimizing Next.js",
};
```

Save the file – if you start the development server and browse the site now, you will see the correct title and description. Moreover, running Lighthouse will now show an improved score, as we've cleared the error!

Excellent – we've seen some examples of the types of warnings or issues that Lighthouse flags and how we might fix them. It's important to understand that this is only a subset based on what Lighthouse flagged for us; there are other areas we should also check, which I will come to in the next section.

The key point here isn't about the specific details: we ran the audit and saw issues appear. I can almost guarantee that no two websites will have the same issues, but you will see similar ones to the ones we've seen here: you won't know what until you try to misappropriate a well-known phrase! As long as you understand what is flagged and can either fix or design it out (so it is no longer an issue), this will be a big step forward in implementing VSO.

Prioritizing the Changes

We have now reached the point where we need to make some decisions – how do we prioritize any issues we see? What other areas should we cover? Both are good questions – let's start with the "other areas." A lot of these you will have already seen at various stages in this book; here is a quick reminder:

- Assessing the framework
- Minimizing HTTP requests
- Enabling browser caching
- Optimizing images
- Utilizing content delivery networks (CDNs)
- Minifying CSS, JavaScript, and HTML
- Using a reliable hosting provider (if not already using a system such as Azure or GitHub/GitLab)
- Trying to capture featured snippets on Google
- Using schema markup
- Optimizing for mobile
- Keeping your site fast

I've not forgotten about others – there are tasks for those outside the developer team, too! Here's a quick reminder, bearing in mind that some of these will require developer help as well:

- Targeting question keywords and other long-tail keywords.

- Using conversational language in your content.

- Prioritizing local SEO.

- Key practices include optimizing meta tags, Open Graph tags, sitemaps, and enhancing page speed.

- Adding FAQ pages.

As we've seen, many of these tasks are designed around page speed, both for desktop and mobile.

There are a few more ideas you can follow up on in this article by Seyed Ahmad on the Dev.to website at `https://dev.to/seyedahmaddv/best-practices-for-seo-optimization-in-nextjs-applications-iad`.

The crunch comes with prioritizing the work – given that every site will be different, there isn't a one-size-fits-all answer, unfortunately! To try to make it easier, let's have a look at some of the questions we can ask:

- If you run the audit, how many areas are affected?

- Are there any quick wins you can achieve with little effort?

- What resources/experience do you have in the wider team for the most critical areas, such as determining keywords to use?

- How up-to-date is your current structured data/meta tag block – is it running at the latest version with only minimal changes needed, or does it require broader, more invasive changes?

In my research, I found an interesting article on this subject at `https://www.dhiwise.com/post/nextjs-seo-essential-strategies` – this could help phase in changes in this area if your website needs more than a minor tweak!

- Content Delivery Networks are a real benefit when it comes to VSO, but you may not have the resources available to implement this: can you do anything quickly that could act as a stopgap?

- In terms of minifying resources, do you already have processes in place to do this, or do you need to add something? Does it require wholesale change, or can something be implemented quickly as a first iteration (i.e., a manual process before fully automating it)?

I'm sure there will be more that we need to answer and that this will lead to some interesting conversations! A lot of what we have covered will be jobs that you have to get on with, making sure that they have appropriate priority in your ticket system and are not simply left to go stale. Hopefully, you will have worked out who can handle the critical stuff and how it can be maintained going forward. The success of VSO will depend on how much you can implement and maintain over time.

Right – let's move on: I've picked out three topics from the whole optimization piece that I want to explore in more detail; this is really to help spark some ideas about what needs to happen and how you can approach the tasks. Two of the three tasks I've chosen are featured snippets and structured data; let's start first with optimizing images.

Implementing Image Changes

Optimizing images should be one of those tasks at the top of any developer's list – depending on how you implement them, it can be anything from inserting a JPEG or PNG file to a WebP or even adding support for SVG images!

It will make illustrating what to do a little complicated, as each site will be different; you will likely have used similar principles if working on multiple sites. We can check a few things that will apply across all sites, so with that in mind, let's run through a few things as part of our next demo.

OPTIMIZING IMAGES

For this next demo, we'll look briefly at the Apress site to see how it stacks up before making changes to the demo site we set up at the beginning of this chapter.

For this demo, I will assume you're using Chrome, but please feel free to use Edge or Firefox if you prefer! I'm still using the homepage, as we did in previous exercises.

To get started, follow these steps:

1. First, let's browse to `https://www.apress.com`, then hit Ctrl+Shift+I to bring up the Developer Console (or use Cmd+Shift+I if using a Mac).

2. Click the Network tab, then hit the Img button to filter out everything else but images.

63

3. If all is well, you should see around 37 items displayed – these
    are the images requested from the server. We can verify this
    by checking the bottom of the Network tab to see the details
    shown in Figure 3-5.

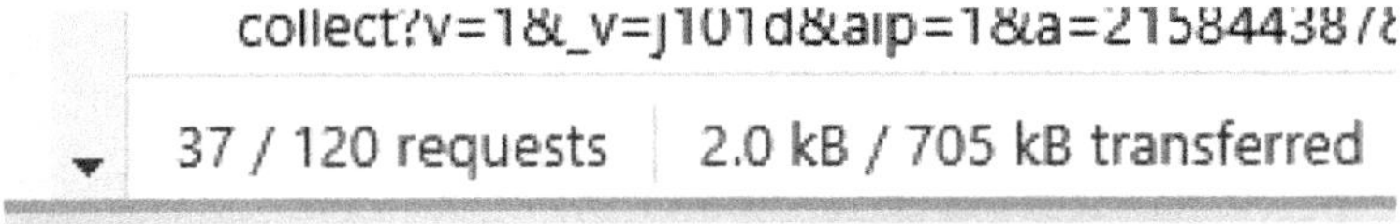

collect?v=1&_v=j101d&aip=1&a=21584438/?

▾   37 / 120 requests   2.0 kB / 705 kB transferred

Figure 3-5. *Total requests loaded, filtered by images*

4. A quick check (Figure 3-6) shows we're calling in 10MB of
    what will be image resources, although a lot of it is coming
    from the cache (shown by the memory cache entries in the Size
    column).

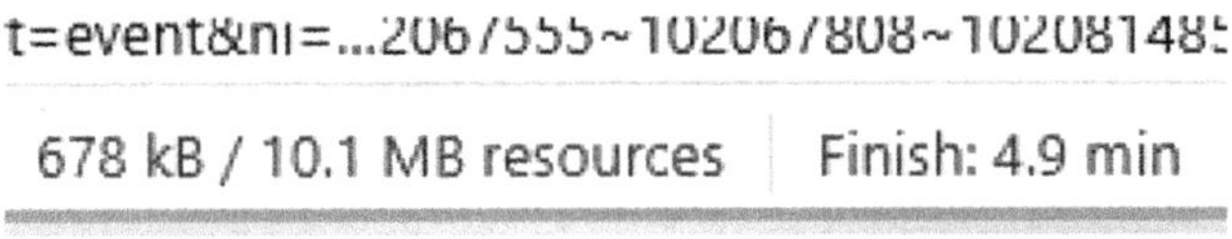

t=event&ni=...206/555~10206/808~102081485

678 kB / 10.1 MB resources   Finish: 4.9 min

Figure 3-6. *Details of total resources loaded for images*

5. Two numbers of interest are Load and DOMContentLoaded –
    the former indicates how long it took to load all of the elements,
    and the Finish value relates to accessing all of the AJAX calls
    needed to render the page (Figure 3-7).

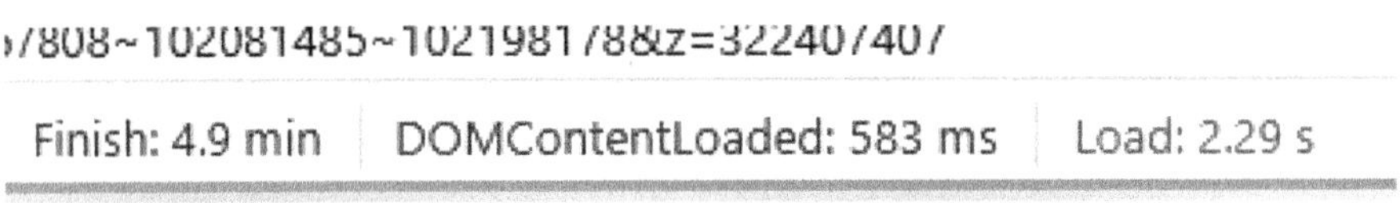

)/808~102081485~1021981/8&z=32240/40/

Finish: 4.9 min   DOMContentLoaded: 583 ms   Load: 2.29 s

Figure 3-7. *The Load and FInish values in the Network tab*

Mmm, this is going to be an interesting one, methinks! Image optimization should be one of those tasks we do as a matter of course, and it will usually be obvious where there is room for improvement. However, in this example, it's not going to be as straightforward – let me explain.

When it comes to optimization, I tend to work to a target of "sub 2 seconds" and hit anything I can to achieve it. In many cases, it's usually pretty obvious where we can make changes, such as switching image formats or shrinking image sizes. However, for the Apress site, if we were optimizing images, I've seen a couple of things that muddy the waters:

1. The Apress homepage loads a lot of image resources (37 in total), but a fair few come from external sources, such as Facebook or Twitter/X. In this instance, we won't be able to change the format used, as it's not under our control.

2. I can see a lot of JPEG and some images that use PNG format. The former works, but it isn't the most compact when it comes to file sizes; it would be better to switch to PNG at a minimum.

3. The Load value is too high – it might only be 2½ seconds, but milliseconds in this day and age count! I think part of the issue here may be that the site uses several external resources from the likes of Facebook and Twitter/X – do we need all of these to be loaded from the front page?

To confirm, you can see the level of support on the CanIUse website at `https://caniuse.com/webp`.

So What Can We Do?

This is an interesting question – I can only go on what I see in the browser, and I'm not a party to anything related to the Apress development process! With that in mind, there are a few things that I have seen – this would be a great example of the kind of thought process we should follow when working through this particular task:

- The first change that comes to mind is image size – could we optimize the images in use? We could do this in one of two ways: by changing the format or running the images through an optimization process. I ran some tests to convert some of the book images from JPEG to WebP format. It gave me a slight reduction of about 3-4Kb, but nothing significant. At the same time, we could try running the images through a compression/optimization process – I did this on one, and it didn't give a massive change, so this might need further investigation.

- I think it would be worth considering lazy loading – given the initial tests haven't (yet) reduced the image sizes, setting the images to only load when needed could reduce the initial load times I've seen in the browser. The slight challenge is that Chrome will complain if lazy loading is used on images that sit above the fold on the initial load, so we might need to be selective about how we implement this! Fortunately, Next.js has lazy loading built-in, so we just need to enable it as a parameter for each image.

- On the subject of image formats, it might be worth looking to see if images could be provided in PNG or WebP format rather than JPEG. It would mean we'd be using a more recent format that would be smaller and quicker to load. If the images are not already on a CDN, then it may be worth looking at implementing one (or the equivalent) to help cache images and make them quicker to load.

- Ordinarily I would consider using the `<picture>` element, but it won't be helpful here. Next.js already provides multiple images in the same way this element works, so we won't gain any benefit. We *could* try switching out the Image component, but we'd lose all of the other benefits that Next.js provides, making the change pointless! The better option would be to use Next's Image component and configure it to work as the HTML5 `<picture>` element works.

- I've also noticed that the home page uses a custom font package similar to FontAwesome. While I know FontAwesome still works for many people, it has been around for a while, and we may find working with pure SVGs better than using a font system. FontAwesome icons are subject to the same styling issues as fonts, making it harder to style; they also have to be imported as an extra resource (albeit only one!). We can add SVGs inline, which makes them faster and removes the need to call for a resource.

There's plenty there for us to think about! It might seem like we've covered a lot of ideas here, but with reason: it's just as important (if not more) to have discussions around what we can do than actually do it so that we stand a chance of success when implementing VSO.

Making Changes to the Demo Site

Optimizing images is one of those tasks that I know not everyone will want to do, but it's a super important part of the maintenance of our site, particularly when it comes to implementing VSO.

Fortunately, if we are using Next.js (as we have done in our demo), then Next.js provides a set of options that helps. It can produce optimized images for different breakpoints, add the lazy loading tag, and set the priority of specific images for rendering on the page.

This is perfect for solving issues such as the flagging for lazy loading on the LCP (or largest content paint) image and lazy loading smaller images in the gallery. Let's look at what we can do as part of the next demo.

UPDATING THE DEMO SITE

To tweak the image setup for our demo site, follow these steps:

1. First, go ahead and open the demo site in your editor.

2. Take copies of the images in the \public folder as backups.

It is not essential, but it is recommended if you want to compare image sizes before and after the change!

---

3. Fire up your browser, then go to https://www. compressjpeg.com, and drag and drop images on the box marked "Drop Your Files Here." Wait for it to complete the process. When it is done, click Download All.

We could use different means to compress – only 2–3 images, so there is no point in implementing something big. If we had more, then implementing it would be good. I'll explore this more in the next section after this demo.

4. Once downloaded, go ahead and add the compressed versions into the \public folder – you may need to rename them so they match the original names or amend the code to suit.

5. The first change we need to make is to add the priority tag to the main image on the homepage at \src\app\page.js – this will remove lazy loading from this picture. Scroll down to the <Image... /> tag shown below, then add the priority tag as indicated:

```
<span className={styles.mainimage}>
  <Image
    src="/ceramics_image.png"
    width={354}
    height={729}
    alt="main illustration"
    priority
  />
</span>
```

6. Save and close page.js. Next, crack open Gallery.js, then amend each of the <Image.../> component calls as shown:

```
<Image
  className="gallery"
  src="/gr1-small.jpg"
  width={130}
```

```
height={126}
blurDataURL="data:image/gif;base64,R0lGOD1hAQABAIAAA
Hd3dwAAACH5BAAAAAAALAAAAAABAAEAAAICRAEAOw=="
alt="Picture of the book"
placeholder="blur"
/>
```

Don't worry about trying to copy the `blurDataURL` tags – the code is in the download!

---

7. Save and close the file. Next, fire up a Node.js terminal session, then change the working folder to the `demo-site` project folder.

8. Enter `npm run dev` at the prompt and press Enter to start the Next.js development server. If all is well, you should see a prompt to confirm the current Next.js version and the URL for localhost – at this point, browse to view your site.

Your site won't look radically different at this point – don't worry: this is to be expected!

The changes are all under the covers; we've told Next that the main image on the home page should have priority (and therefore load normally), plus we'll see blurred gray images for the gallery page. These changes have highlighted some interesting points for further discussion, so let's go through them in more detail.

Exploring the Changes

So, what did we achieve in the last demo?

We may have only made some minor changes to the site in this demo, but it (at least for me) highlighted one thing: if we're using Next.js, we need to spend time in the documentation, particularly around the next/image component!

Why? Well, Next.js has spent a lot of time adding to and perfecting its image component, so it now automatically optimizes sizes, lazy loads by default, supports features such as blurring on initial load, and more.

We saw at least one issue appearing for images in our demo when checking through Lighthouse:

Above-the-fold images that are lazily loaded render later in the page lifecycle, which can delay the largest contentful paint.

This issue is an easy fix (or so I thought) – Next.js has a priority flag you can add, which sets the image to be preloaded in the markup, as shown in Figure 3-8.

```
nomodule></script>
<link rel="preload" as="image" imagesrcset="/_nex
t/image?url=%2Fceramics_image.png&w=384&q=75 1x,
/_next/image?url=%2Fceramics_image.png&w=750&q=75
2x"> == $0
```

Figure 3-8. *Preloading an image in Next.js*

We had to do this for the main ceramics image on the home page, as it so happens to be the LCP element on that page, plus delaying a large image on load will harm the user experience.

For the second change, we added a blurring option to show a low-res image on the initial load before switching to the final version. This feature is good for helping speed up loading times, although we'll only see the real impact once we push the code out to production. We can see an example of the code added in this excerpt from our demo, where I've highlighted the changes in bold:

```
<Image
  className="gallery"
  src="/gr3-small.jpg"
  width={130}
  height={126}
  blurDataURL="data:image/gif;base64,R0lGODlhAQABAIAAAHd3dwAAA
  CH5BAAAAAAALAAAAAABAAEAAAICRAEAOw=="
  alt="Picture of the book"
  placeholder="blur"
/>
```

For reference, you must add the `blur` option and the low-res data image under the `blurDataURL` tag for this feature to work.

You will see from the code base that I've not optimized how images are displayed. There is scope to do more, like converting the HTML markup for the gallery component to only show one instance and using it to loop through an array of image properties. I've shown the code as a starting point for now, but I would expect to pick this up as part of any future optimization work!

It's at this point while writing this book that I thought this would be enough – the documentation said adding the priority tag was enough for the LCP issue and that adding the blur would be good should we push it into production. Unfortunately, fate would seem to suggest otherwise.

A Sting in the Tale

When I added the priority tag for the LCP issue, I got another warning, which I've displayed in Figure 3-9.

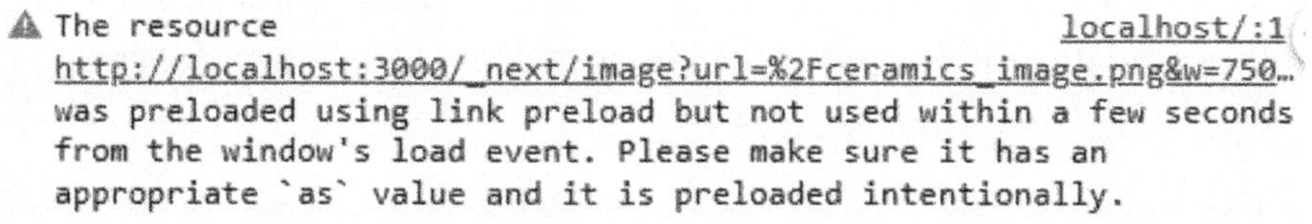

```
⚠ The resource                               localhost/:1
  http://localhost:3000/_next/image?url=%2Fceramics_image.png&w=750…
  was preloaded using link preload but not used within a few seconds
  from the window's load event. Please make sure it has an
  appropriate `as` value and it is preloaded intentionally.
```

Figure 3-9. *Warning displayed in the browser for preload issue*

I've replicated the text for easier reading below:

The resource <NAME OF IMAGE> was preloaded using link preload but not used within a few seconds from the window's load event. Please make sure it has an appropriate `as` value and it is preloaded intentionally.

While this in itself didn't seem too odd, it did throw up a bit of a sting in the tail, which I'm still unsure about! The documentation states that we should just need to add the priority tag, but it seems this wasn't enough – at least in this case. I ended up having to add this to the next configuration.mjs file:

```
const nextConfig = {
  images: {
    unoptimized: true,
  },
};
```

It seems to have stopped the error from coming – I can only imagine that Chrome was seeing an issue with priority not being set for one or more of the image set it created automatically for the ceramics image. I wouldn't consider this a final fix, as we've not done anything around specifying image sizes for different platforms – it's worth investigating!

As an aside, if you are using Next.js, then I would strongly recommend reading through the documentation for its Image component at `https://nextjs.org/docs/pages/building-your-application/optimizing/images`, as I am sure it will bring up points for further discussion. One document of particular note will be this one, relating to image sizes for different platforms: `https://nextjs.org/docs/app/api-reference/components/image#devicesizes`.

I've also seen links online pointing to what looks like a useful image optimizer for Next.js at `https://www.npmjs.com/package/next-image-export-optimizer`. If we had more images, then automating more of the process would undoubtedly be something to consider in future development.

Okay, let's move on: we mentioned something way back in Chapter 1 called featured snippets. Remember them? This is where Google will show a short snippet of text from your site if it answers a question entered as a search term.

Adding featured snippets is essential to implementing VSO, but ironically, we can't do anything *specific* for it! It might sound a little odd, so let's dive in and look at this in more detail.

Adding Featured Snippets

Cast your mind back to Chapter 1 – do you remember us asking Google how to create a cappuccino and that it gave us the response shown in Figure 3-10?

A classic cappuccino calls for **1/3 espresso, 1/3 steamed milk, and 1/3 foam**. You can mix it up by using 2 or 3 tablespoons of flavored syrups or even different kinds of milk, like chocolate or vanilla. You can sprinkle some cocoa powder or cinnamon on top of the frothed milk for an extra touch of flavor.

F   Folgers Coffee
    https://www.folgerscoffee.com › coffee › how-to-guides   ⋮   ✅

How to Make Cappuccino - Folgers Coffee

❓ About featured snippets   •   🔖 Feedback

Figure 3-10.   *A reminder of how to make cappuccinos*

It's important to understand that while featured snippets are a key part of VSO, we can't set them up explicitly but complete tasks elsewhere that will help influence whether a featured snippet will display. Let me explain what I mean.

The key to displaying a featured snippet lies almost entirely with Google – they will decide whether to display content from our site as a featured snippet in its search results. At present, no publicly available information shows details of the algorithm used by Google to determine what to display – it means that we're in the lap of the gods when it comes to knowing if it will use our content! However, we can make changes to help improve the chances of displaying content as a featured snippet from our site.

Many of these tasks are ones we should be doing for standard SEO as a matter of course – the difference here, though, is that the type of content will differ. For example, we will use the long-tail type discussed in Chapter 1 instead of single keywords. I've put together a table of tasks in Table 3-1.

Table 3-1. *Strategies for optimizing for featured snippets*

Task	Tasks and Notes
Identify potential snippet opportunities	Conduct keyword research to identify queries likely to trigger feature snippets Look for long-tail keywords and questions that align with your content
Structure your content for clarity	Structure your content into clear, concise answers to improve readability Use headings and bullet points in numbered lists to create step-by-step instructions
Use the inverted pyramid style	Use an inverted pyramid style of writing, presenting the most critical information first; content will deliver more value, which increases capturing the snippet spot
Optimize metadata	Optimize page titles and meta descriptions for target queries. It doesn't directly influence snippet selection but helps to improve overall SEO performance and click-through rates
Leverage schema markup	Use schema markup and structured data to help search engines understand your content and increase its chances of appearing as a search snippet. Add schema types like FAQ, How-To, and Q&A for extra context

Many of these tasks will be ones we need to do for traditional SEO – the trick here will be to adapt *what* we define as queries and markup to include queries that better match what we need for VSO.

This is why it's so essential for SEO individuals and developers to work closely together. SEO individuals can provide the static content required for each page, but it will be down to developers to see if they can source it from the back-end data.

A great example would be product pages – content such as product names and IDs should be available in the back end so we can use them dynamically based on what the SEO team provides as static content. As long as the content is present and accurate and we're using valid and semantic markup, this will help improve our chances with Google.

Okay, let's crack on: as part of working toward implementing featured snippets, we need to set up structured data and the appropriate meta tags. It is an easy change in Next.js (assuming you're using version 15), but it requires guidance from the SEO experts to provide the right content! To see what I mean, let's take a look at updating the demo site to use this block and explore some examples of how we can customize it for our needs.

Implementing Structured Data and Meta Tags

One of the key elements of setting up VSO and optimizing our site is adding structured data to each page's head. I touched on this briefly back in Chapter 1 – what does it do?

The best way to describe this is that it's a standardized format for providing information about any page and its content. It helps search engines better understand your content on a page so they can deliver more relevant results to users.

It is typically implemented using JSON-LD (JavaScript Object Notation for Linked Data), a method of encoding Linked Data using JSON.

There is a catch – although we may use JSON-LD, the method for implementing it will vary: this depends on whether you are serving static or dynamic content. Let's dive into a quick demo that adds both types to our demo site to show you what I mean.

Please be aware that this demo will use Next.js version 15; there have been a lot of changes around how Next.js handles this type of data in previous versions, so the code here may not work in earlier versions!

IMPLEMENTING STRUCTURED DATA – STATIC AND DYNAMIC CONTENT

For this demo, I will use the demo-site demo we created earlier and assume you are still using Google as your browser. To set the structured data content for our site, follow these steps:

1. First, crack open the page.js file at the root of the /src/app folder, then add this constant, which defines some values for the <head> element of the page:

    ```
    export const metadata = {
      title: "Demo Site for Optimization",
      name: "description",
      description: "This is a demo site for optimizing
      Next.js",
    };
    ```

2. Save the file, then switch to a Node.js terminal session.

3. At the prompt, make sure you are in the demo-site project folder; if not, change to it.

4. Enter npm run dev, and press enter to start the Next.js development server.

5. Browse to http://localhost:3000, then press Ctrl+Shift+I to bring up the development console (or Cmd+Shift+I if using a Mac). Switch to the Elements tab, then expand the <head> section. If all is well, we should see something similar to Figure 3-11.

```
<script src="/_next/static/chunks/app/layout.js" async></script>
<title>Demo Site for Optimization</title>
<meta name="description" content="This is a demo site for optimizing Next.js">
<link rel="icon" href="/favicon.ico" type="image/x-icon" sizes="16x16">
```

Figure 3-11. *Example of structured data for static content*

Okay, we now have a version in place for static content. If, however, we want to implement it for dynamic content (such as product pages), we need to use a different method. Let's take a look at the changes we need to make:

6. Revert to your editor, then comment out the `metadata ={…}` block; we don't want this to show.

7. Go ahead and add these two blocks of code:

```
export const product = {
  name: "ceramics",
  image: "./gr1-small.jpg",
  description: "test description for ceramics",
};

const jsonLd = {
  "@context": "https://schema.org",
  "@type": "Product",
  name: product.name,
  image: product.image,
  description: product.description,
};
```

I've hardwired both for now, but there's a reason; I will return to this shortly.

8. Scroll down to the bottom of the page, then add this block
   before the closing </> fragment tag:

```
<Script
    id="structured-data-script"
    type="application/ld+json"
    dangerouslySetInnerHTML={{ __html: JSON.
    stringify(jsonLd) }}
/>

</>
```

9. You will notice that we call the Script component from Next.js;
   this will fail due to <Script...> not being recognized. To fix
   it, we need to add this line at the top to import the component:

```
import Script from "next/script";
```

10. Save and close the file.

11. Next, switch to a Node.js terminal session, then change the
    working folder to the demo-site folder. Enter npm run dev to
    restart the dev server at the prompt, and press Enter.

12. Go ahead and browse to http://localhost:3000/ – if all
    is good, you should see structured data appear in the browser
    console, similar to that shown in Figure 3-12.

```
▼ <script id="structured-data-script" type="application/ld+json" data-nscript="afterInterac
  tive">
    {"@context":"https://schema.org","@type":"Product","name":"ceramics","image":"./gr1-
    small.jpg","description":"test description for ceramics"}
  </script>
```

Figure 3-12. *An example of structured data for dynamic content*

Excellent – we now have the means to add structured data; we use the JSON-LD format in both cases, but the how varies depending on whether we're displaying static or dynamic content. This demo has highlighted some interesting concepts, so let's take a moment to review the changes in more detail.

Understanding the Changes

I'm not usually a betting man *per se*, but when it comes to working on anything that involves that behemoth known as Google, I'll take every helping hand I can get!

Adding a structured data block as part of optimizing for VSO is one such helping hand – this tells Google (and the other search engines) more about our site so it can deliver more targeted results. To do this, we have to use one of two ways, depending on whether you are working with static or dynamic content on your page.

In our demo, we first added a static block of tags, which we wrapped in a metadata constant. Next.js is designed to detect and use this block automatically, so we only need to specify the appropriate tags within it. To prove this, we ran up the development server to preview the results displayed in the <head> section of the homepage.

In this demo, we only added a couple of properties, but there are more we could add – for details, please see the documentation on the main Next.js website at `https://nextjs.org/docs/app/building-your-application/optimizing/metadata`.

When it comes to dynamic content, this requires a little more work and brings a bit more risk – we can't use the metadata block as before. Instead, we have to use the Script component from Next.js to manually insert a `dangerouslySetInnerHTML` tag in a block at the bottom of the page. We first set up a demo product object that contains some dummy data; we then pulled it into the jsonLd JSON object that contains the @context, @type, name, image, and description blocks.

I hardcoded the product const with some dummy data to call specific properties such as product.description. It is enough to simulate dynamic data's appearance; I'll return to this shortly.

The critical part we add at the end of the page is the call to the <Script...> component, where we specify the id value, type, and set dangerouslySetInnerHTML to render a stringified version of the JSON block. The risk here is that if we had used just innerHTML, we would inject the DOM with live HTML, which could expose us to an XSS attack if we're not careful. Instead, using dangerouslysetInnerHTML renders the values as plain text, reducing the risk of attack. We then ran up the Next.js development server to verify that it added the structured data at the bottom of the page of our site. So, what's the story with dynamic data?

I mentioned just now that I had hardcoded the (simulated) properties for the dynamic block – in reality, we'd keep the jsonLd block and replace the "hardcoded" values with those called from our backend source. To see what this would look like, below is an example that uses a getProduct() function to call for our data and pass it into a product object. We can then, in turn, use this in the jsonLd block, similar to what we did just now:

```
export default async function Page({ params }) {
  const product = await getProduct(params.id)

  const jsonLd = {
    '@context': 'https://schema.org',
    '@type': 'Product',
    name: product.name,
```

```
      image: product.image,
      description: product.description,
    }
  return (
    <section>
      {/* Add JSON-LD to your page */}
      <script
        type="application/ld+json"
        dangerouslySetInnerHTML={{ __html: JSON.stringify
        (jsonLd) }}
      />
      {/*... */}
    </section>
  )
}
```

We could have used a function like getServerSideProps() from
Next.js to get our data, but either would have worked fine. The critical
bit is that we have a means to call the required data and pass it into
the jsonLd object so we can render it in a similar way to the static
data block.

Okay, let's crack on – there is one topic I suspect most developers
loathe, but with the advent of upcoming legislation, I know it's one we
must touch on! It's another area that is super critical to implementing VSO,
so let's dive in and take a look.

83

Assessing Support for Mobile

Mobile support.

Yes, this is the topic I know many developers hate, as it introduces a raft of complexities to any design. The trouble is that with so many people accessing the Internet via mobile devices, we can't simply ignore them, so we have to make sure our site works on as many platforms as is reasonably practical.

At this point, things get complicated: the first decision we must make is which devices we support? The simple answer is that a check of analytics software will show the most commonly used ones; this requires a discussion with the product owner and analytics people to decide which to support.

Leaving that aside, we can use the Lighthouse scanner tool again to test the same areas; this time, it will throttle for mobile devices. As part of our next demo, let's run through the tool again to see what it shows for mobile devices.

Bear in mind that you won't get precisely the same results as me – this is more about the principles of testing, not the result!

TESTING FOR MOBILE SUPPORT

To assess both the example site and my demo site for mobile support, follow these steps – you will see that we're doing much the same as we did back at the start of this chapter, but this time focusing on Mobile:

1. First, fire up your browser and head to Apress's main website, at `https://www.apress.com`.

2. Press F12 or Ctrl+Shift+I to bring up the Developer Console, and click the Lighthouse tab.

3. Hit the Mobile option under Device, then click Analyze page load to the right. Wait for it to complete the test.

4. When the test is complete, you will see something akin to the result shown in Figure 3-13.

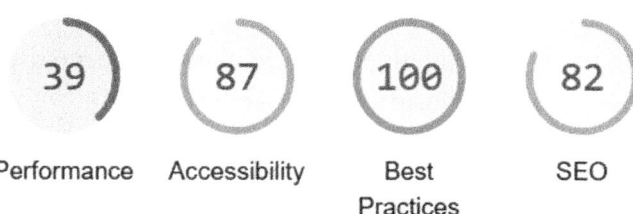

Figure 3-13. *Results of the Lighthouse test for the Apress site (Mobile)*

5. Next, fire up a Node.js terminal session, then change the working folder to the demo site we created at the start of this chapter.

6. At the prompt, enter npm run dev and press Enter – this will start the Next.js development server.

7. Repeat steps two to four to get the results for the demo site in Desktop conditions.

8. If all is well, you should see something akin to those shown in Figure 3-14.

Figure 3-14. *Results of the Lighthouse test for my demo site (Mobile)*

Mmm, there are some interesting results there, with some wide differences and scope for improvement!

In this last demo, we ran a very similar test to the one we did earlier in the chapter – digging into the results shows a few areas where we need to work, but also that there is some crossover between mobile and desktop when it comes to issues flagged by Lighthouse. Let's take a moment to dig into them in more detail to understand what issues we might have to fix and where fixing one platform will help fix the other.

Digging into the Detail

One thing I love about Lighthouse is that it is one of those tools that can generate lots of conversation!

What do I mean by this? Well, running the tool is a simple affair: it's what comes at the results stage that might provoke those discussions. It was certainly true on this particular run, where the results showed some crossover with Desktop and some interesting possibilities for Mobile. Let's take a look at both of the results, starting with my demo site.

Analyzing the Demo Site

Cast your mind back to the beginning of this chapter, when we ran the Lighthouse audit for Desktop. Do you remember some of the issues that it flagged? A good example is the need to minify JavaScript; it should be no surprise that the Mobile audit also flagged the same issue!

Note – I've only listed issues from audits where the result was less than 100%, so we will only see a few examples.

This issue isn't the only one it flagged, so I've listed the top candidates from that audit in Table 3-2.

Table 3-2. *Results of the Mobile audit for the demo site*

Audit	Issue or Warning Flagged
Performance	Serve images in next-gen formats
	Minify JavaScript
	Reduce unused JavaScript
	Page preventing back/forward cache restoration
	Largest Contentful Paint element
	Tweak payloads to be smaller in size
Best Practices	Serve images with low resolution
	Ensure CSP is effective against XSS attacks
	Missing source maps for large first-party JavaScript
SEO	Document doesn't have a `<title>` element
	Document does not have a meta description

At first glance, this seems like a reasonable set of issues to deal with; we already saw some of these when running the same tests for Desktop. For example, I'm not surprised about the "Serve images in next-gen formats," as a similar issue arose earlier in this chapter. Some of these are easy to fix, such as the `<title>` element, whereas others, like the CSP policy, require a little more work.

However, we are potentially missing a bigger issue with this site: the mobile version isn't exactly … well … mobile! Let me explain what I mean.

Let's assume you have the demo site running in a browser under `http://localhost:3000`, as we've done before in the tests. If you hit Ctrl+Shift+I and then Ctrl+Shift+M to enter Responsive mode, you might see something akin to that shown in Figure 3-15. Mmm, it's not exactly responsive, is it?

Figure 3-15. *The demo site, displayed in iPhone 12 Pro mobile view*

In an ideal world, we would follow a mobile-first approach, meaning that the above design would appear a lot more polished than it is! However, what we have here does help illustrate an important point – some of the issues we see are related to the current poor design and are not fixable until we revamp it.

For example, we already know that the front page has a large image of ceramics, which is our Large Content Paint element – this is effectively invisible on the initial load. We need to rework where this is displayed first, then update the `<Image...>` component to render a smaller version as part of the image source set. In a similar vein, we are also seeing issues flagged for JavaScript – we should investigate whether we can rationalize how much is used for legacy browsers and work on reducing the payload sizes so that the site loads faster in a mobile browser.

As an aside, the mobile analysis has brought up the need to add a sitemap – this didn't appear in previous audits, hence showing that Lighthouse can be a little variable at times! I will cover this a little later in this chapter.

Okay, let's switch focus and have a look at what the Lighthouse audit for the Apress website flagged. Based on the previous run, I expect we would have more work to do, but who knows?

Analyzing the Apress Site

As it happens, I wasn't wrong – Lighthouse indeed flagged a few issues requiring attention!

Okay, to be fair, it's not something we will be able to rectify in the course of these pages, but it's still worth a look at what kind of issues were flagged and whether we could do anything about them. As before, we'll begin with the Performance audit:

- Avoiding large layout shifts

- LCP element issues

- Eliminating render-blocking resources

- Reducing unused and minifying JavaScript code

- Minifying CSS

- Serving next-gen images

In terms of SEO, it flagged two issues, which we've seen before:

- Links are not crawlable.

- Document doesn't have a valid hreflang.

It is an interesting set of results – Apress's website shows signs that it supports mobile better than our demo site, but we still have issues with performance. If we were to fix the issues, then there are a few things I can see that would be easy wins as a starting point:

- Check the LCP: this was flagged due to an issue with the home page banner – could this be compressed, or could a smaller size be used?

- Dig into the JavaScript used on the site: can we minify the code used or reduce it by only targeting more recent browsers? Can we do something similar for CSS?

- Serving next-gen image formats: given that WebP has good browser support, can we not use this format where possible?

I, of course, don't have the answers, but that's not the point of this exercise – it's all about getting the right people together, having those discussions, and prioritizing what people think will be the right changes at the right time!

A Postscript

Before we move on to accessibility, there are two things I want to cover: adding a sitemap and considering automating the Lighthouse procedure. Let's have a look at the sitemap first.

When I ran the Lighthouse audits as part of researching for this book, I discovered that it started to flag up an issue around a missing sitemap. This lack of sitemap wasn't unexpected, as I hadn't put anything in place, but as it so happens, it's an essential part of optimizing for VSO!

Fortunately, it's easy to implement one for Next.js version 15. Let's take a look at how it will be part of our next demo.

ADDING A SITEMAP

To implement a sitemap on our site, follow these steps:

1. First, crack open the demo-site project in your editor if you don't already have it running.

2. Create a new file in the \src\app folder, and call it sitemap.js. Go ahead and add this code:

```
export default function sitemap() {
  return [
    {
      url: "http://localhost:3000",
      lastModified: new Date(),
      changeFrequency: "yearly",
      priority: 1,
    },
  ];

}
```

3. Next, switch to a Node.js terminal session, then make sure the working folder is set to the demo-site folder.

4. Enter npm run dev at the prompt, and press Enter to start the Next.js development server.

5.   Browse to `http://localhost:3000/sitemap.xml`, then wait a couple of moments: if all is well, we should see a sitemap appear similar to that shown in Figure 3-16.

```
▼<urlset xmlns="http://www.sitemaps.org/schemas/sitemap/0.9">
  ▼<url>
     <loc>http://localhost:3000</loc>
     <lastmod>2025-01-25T14:48:07.127Z</lastmod>
     <changefreq>yearly</changefreq>
     <priority>1</priority>
  </url>
</urlset>
```

Figure 3-16. *The newly created sitemap for our demo site*

That was an easy change – probably one of our easier ones! I know you'll probably say, "But we should already have one in place, right?" and the answer should be a resounding yes. Please don't forget that this is a demo site, though, so not everything will be present – the key to this demo is to understand that we need *something* in place and that we style it appropriately as part of our optimization work.

There is one more thought I want to leave you with before we look at accessibility – that question about automating the Lighthouse audit process. We've already seen that Lighthouse has identified some important changes we need to make, even though we've only checked one page.

The right thing to do would be to implement Lighthouse in the CI pipeline so this check is done automatically and set to pass or fail as appropriate. I recommend searching for "implementing lighthouse in a ci pipeline" on Google. There are plenty of articles that take you through the process!

Okay, let's move on: we have one more task for this chapter, which is that dreaded word "accessibility"! Yes, I know – it's that topic we all have to consider.

Assessing Accessibility

Auditing your site is crucial to maintaining any site, whether it be a greenfield offer or something that has matured over several years (and probably reaching a point where it should be retired!).

It can be a double-edged sword, though: on the one hand, we're making the site more open to those who have health challenges such as deuteranopia or a physical disability, which makes using a PC difficult. The flip side is that if an issue such as color contrast is flagged, this might require UX changes that conflict with your existing branding, and we can't easily fix it without more widespread changes!

Whatever the outcome, we have to run an audit first. For convenience, we'll use the same tool as before; I'll return to this at the end of the chapter. Let's dive in and take a look at what we have in more detail.

ASSESSING ACCESSIBILITY

To check our site for accessibility, run these steps:

1. First, fire up your browser, and head to Apress's main website, at `https://www.apress.com`.

2. Press F12 or Ctrl+Shift+I to bring up the Developer Console, and click the Lighthouse tab.

3. Hit the Desktop option under Device, then click Analyze page load to the right. Wait for it to complete the test.

4. When the test is complete, you will see something akin to the result shown in Figure 3-17.

Figure 3-17. *Results of the Lighthouse test for the Apress site (Desktop)*

5. Click the no entry symbol to clear the report, then hit Mobile I Analyze to rerun the same audit for Mobile.

6. Next, fire up a Node.js terminal session, then change the working folder to the demo site we created at the start of this chapter.

7. At the prompt, enter `npm run dev`, and press Enter – this will start the Next.js development server.

8. Repeat steps two to four to get the results for the demo site in Desktop conditions.

9. Once done, clear the report as before, then repeat the same steps to audit the site for Mobile.

Excellent – we've now run our initial tests for accessibility! The sharp-eyed among you will notice that we've already done something similar but for different reasons. It isn't an issue: Lighthouse never returns consistent results each time, so it's best to work on iterative audits until everything appears at 100%.

We also need to run these tests periodically – I will return to this at the end of the demo.

This time, the results returned show a couple of issues of concern but nothing we can't fix. The irony here is that if we had run the same tests elsewhere on each site, the same fixes would rectify issues there, too – such as the missing `<title>` element. Let's keep that in mind while we take a closer look at the issues flagged in this demo.

Reviewing the Results

Cast your mind back to earlier in the chapter – I know, it seems long ago! – where we ran our first Lighthouse audit. It covered four areas: Performance, Best Practices, SEO, and the one we're interested in – Accessibility.

This time, we ran it for all four platforms to cover Desktop and Mobile for the localhost demo site and Apress as our sample. We didn't get a clear 100% result for any environment, but the results were pretty close at around 87-91%!

Fortunately, we got the same results each for Desktop and Mobile for the localhost site, so fixing one will fix the other; the same applies to Apress, but we had slightly more results that we would have to rectify. Let's look at each in turn, starting with the results for our demo site, which I've listed in Table 3-3.

Table 3-3. *The Accessibility audit results for our demo site*

Issue Flagged	Details
Document doesn't have a `<title>` element	This issue is simple to fix – we need to add that title element! It would probably be done as part of the structured data work anyway, although we must be mindful of whether it has to contain dynamic content, such as a product name
`<html>` element does not have a `[lang]` attribute	This one is probably a little tricker for some sites – it will depend on whether we support English or need to support other languages (and by how many) We'll be looking at internationalization for VSO in Chapter 5

We had a few more items flagged for the Apress site, even though we won't be able to fix them! It doesn't matter – it's still important to see examples of what *could* be flagged to know what type of issues to expect. Let's look at the results for the Apress site, which I've listed in Table 3-4.

Table 3-4. *The Accessibility audit results for the Apress site*

Issue Flagged	Details
`<frame>` or `<iframe>` elements do not have a title	This issue should be simple to fix – Hayden Barnes's video is missing a title property, so we need to specify one with the video to pass accessibility

Links do not have a discernible name	This is being flagged as all links need to have text or a description in an `aria-label` to pass accessibility checks. In our case, we have two links that have failed the check:
	 `A.abstract.internal`
	 `A.footer__meta__logo`
	 Adding the tag is a snap, but deciding what to put in and how will require more effort!

Heading elements are not in a sequentially descending order	This may be trickier to solve – heading elements should flow from H1 down to H6, but it looks like the code jumps straight to H3 and skips out H1 and H2 tags. The easy option would be to change H3 to H1, but we have a heavily nested `<div>` structure, which isn't the easiest to read! Instead, we might have to change to a `<div>` or `<span>` and restyle it accordingly

These three issues are not the only ones that Lighthouse flagged. I've pulled out one extra, as it shows there may be more to an issue than it initially appears. The issue in question is this one:

```
Links rely on color to be distinguishable
```

... which is being flagged on two p elements and two external links. Although non-disabled people can see this is a link, it is not easy to see in some environments, mainly when using a screen reader. Take a look at the highlighted section of text shown in Figure 3-18.

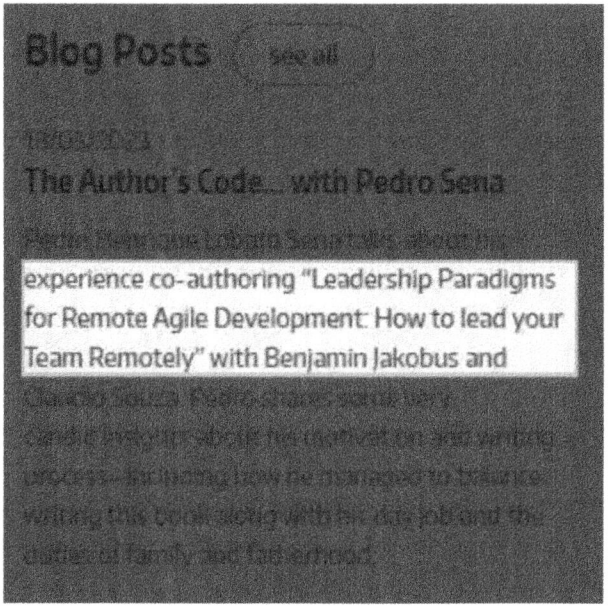

Figure 3-18. *Highlighted text for discernable link issue*

The issue is that we have a link present, but there is insufficient contrast between the colors used on ordinary text and those used for links. This is where it gets tricky.

The simple fix is to change the colors used for regular links, but at the same time, check active, hover, focused, and (potentially) disabled link colors, too, so they all fit in with current branding. However, we must ensure all link colors have a contrast ratio of at least 3:1, similar to the example shown in Figure 3-19.

Figure 3-19. *An example of contrast ratio*

The catch here is that it seems the `is-external` external classes against at least one failing element, but they don't appear in the stylesheet! It means it's difficult to tell what the contrast ratio is at present, so not only do we need to change the color(s), but we should also include the missing external styles in the stylesheet so we can be sure they do not fall foul of this ratio check.

Taking Next Steps

Testing our site using the in-built Lighthouse audit tool is helpful, as it gives a quick and dirty indication of where we might have issues.

However, it's not a sustainable option for larger websites – it would take too long to keep checking each page! At the same time, we may also be running it prematurely; at least one of the issues Lighthouse flagged was for a missing title element, which could well have been added when we had set up the structured data block earlier in the chapter. It wasn't a deliberate omission on my part, but it shows that running Lighthouse at the right point makes sense, not just every time you make a change.

To fix this issue, we should consider automating the checking process – fortunately, Lighthouse allows us to push it into a CI pipeline, so it can run each time we push up code. There are some added benefits to automating the process:

- Running automatic checks means we can configure when this happens: it makes sense to do it once the code is submitted and reviewed, not while it's still liable to change!

- We get a more accurate view of any issues across the whole site, not just on a single page, and can apply a fix across all instances of an issue, not just in one location.

- We can take things further by implementing axe, a tool for testing accessibility (from `https://www.deque.com/axe-accessibility-testing-tools/`). Some plugins allow us to integrate it with unit tests simultaneously, making our code even more resilient.

To give you an example of what is possible, I asked ChatGPT to detail the process for implementing the axe tool with the Cypress testing suite. I know this is probably cheating a little, but in this day and age, AI is playing an increasing role in development, and there is no sense in reinventing the wheel if someone else has already done it!

I've included a PDF that shows the type of code we could use. It's a theoretical example that could potentially be a starting point for further development – it will show you what's involved and hopefully give you something to work with on future projects.

Great – there's one last point I want to cover before we move on to the next chapter: tactics for ensuring website accessibility.

While initially researching for this book, I used ChatGPT to detail some of the challenges we might face when optimizing for VSO. It came back with some interesting information, including a checklist for checking website accessibility (Table 3-5).

Table 3-5. *Tactics for optimizing accessibility*

Tactic	Detail
Follow WCAG Standards	Adhere to the Web Content Accessibility (WCAG) POUR Guidelines
Use Alt Text and Descriptive Metadata	Write descriptive and informative alt text for all images optimized for search engines
Implement Semantic HTML	Use proper HTML5 semantic elements to create logical content hierarchies that assist screen readers and improve voice search interpretation
Ensure Keyboard Navigation	Design your site so all functions are accessible via keyboard to improve overall site usability, particularly for those unable to use a mouse
Test with Assistive Technologies	Regularly test your site with tools such as screen readers and voice assistants to identify and address accessibility gaps
Accessible Forms and Input Fields	Ensure forms have clear labels, proper focus indicators, and error messages that are both visually and programmatically discernible
Optimize for Mobile Accessibility	Test accessibility on mobile devices to ensure it passes – pay particular attention to using larger touch targets and avoid elements that require precision gestures
Provide Text Alternatives	Include text descriptions or downloadable resources for any non-text content (e.g., charts, infographics)
Enable Text Resizing	Allow users to resize text up to 200% without breaking your site's layout or functionality
Test Frequently	Perform accessibility audits with tools like Axe or Lighthouse and involve users with disabilities in usability testing to gain authentic feedback

While it's important to remember some precautions we must take with ChatGPT-generated content, there are some valuable tips in this list and ones we would do well to bring into day-to-day site maintenance! I know that not all developers will be cognizant of some of the details in checking for accessibility, so this is a great way to get into the mindset of checking for accessibility compliance during the development process.

Summary

Phew – what a monster chapter!

Optimizing a site is undoubtedly one of the most critical tasks in development, yet it often takes a back seat as teams do not always see it as a priority! Implementing VSO is a good excuse to change this, as many of the tasks we would otherwise complete as part of maintenance are required for VSO. Throughout this chapter, we've covered a lot of useful tips around some of these tasks, so let's take a moment to review what we have learned.

We started way back with setting up what will be the demo site for this chapter and one we'd use as a basis for learning about optimizing – we swiftly followed with a look at some of the challenges around React/Next.js and SEO and what can affect voice search optimization.

Next up, we got stuck into running Lighthouse so we could understand what sort of issues we might see – we covered that issues may not always be the same on each audit but that it's more important to iterate until we can either fix or design out any issues that show in the audit. We focused on the performance and SEO points for now, as accessibility would come later in the chapter.

With our audit done, we then moved on to implementing changes. At this point, we focused on those we could do on the demo site, such as adding featured snippets, structuring data, and optimizing images. We then switched to assessing support for mobile devices and noted that our demo site needed more work – not unexpected! We also looked at Apress's site to get a feel for what to expect as a comparison in terms of performance, SEO, and mobile support.

To finish things off, we reran the audits, but this time focused on just accessibility. We noted that using Lighthouse will give us some good pointers, but it isn't the most effective use of resources. We learned that automating the process would be a better use of time, an example of which is in the accompanying PDF.

Okay, let's move on: it's time to spice things up a little! Search engine optimization has always been about improving the search experience, so our site lands a little higher in the search results, making it easier for customers to find. We've discussed the need to use longer phrases when searching (as part of VSO), but we haven't explored the V part of VSO: Voice. Time to change that – stay with me, and I will reveal all in the next chapter.

CHAPTER 4

Adding Speech Capabilities

Up until now, we've touched on a variety of topics that make up voice search optimization, such as optimizing for speed or adding structured data and tags – you'd be forgiven for thinking we've started a journey across what can only be a minefield of different things that we need to do!

We've already talked about the need to use long-tail keywords when searching. Instead of entering these manually, why not use the power of voice to enter them vocally? Over the following few pages, we will explore how to add speech capabilities to a search facility so you can articulate any terms without the need to type.

Speaking is a more natural way to articulate what we need when searching, so combining this and the search facility into one component makes sense! Think about it – anyone who owns a smart device, such as Siri or Alexa, will do this anyway, so why can't we have it on a website, too?

Getting Started

Searching for something by voice opens a whole host of possibilities – people with disabilities will likely do this anyway, but this shouldn't limit us: current technology allows us to replicate the same effect on websites today.

To show you what this would look like, we can start with something easy – if you own a (recent) Android phone, you can do this using Google.

© Alex Libby 2025
A. Libby, *Beginning Voice Search Optimization*, Design Thinking,
https://doi.org/10.1007/979-8-8688-1841-7_4

The same effect should also work on iPhones: I confess that being a diehard Android user, I tend to favor using that platform! That aside, let's dig in and find out how we can search using Google on a phone, using our voice:

USING GOOGLE VOICE SEARCH

To search using voice, follow these steps:

1. First, we need to fire up the Google app on a cell phone – you should see the regular search box; inside this box, look for a microphone symbol.

2. Tap the symbol – this opens the microphone, ready for use. You'll see your Google app set to listen, as shown in Figure 4-1, where I've highlighted the Listening face and 4-bar "equalizer."

Listening...

Figure 4-1. *The Google app set to listen*

3. At the bottom of the screen, you will see some previous searches – these are not necessarily yours but could be ones of interest (Figure 4-2).

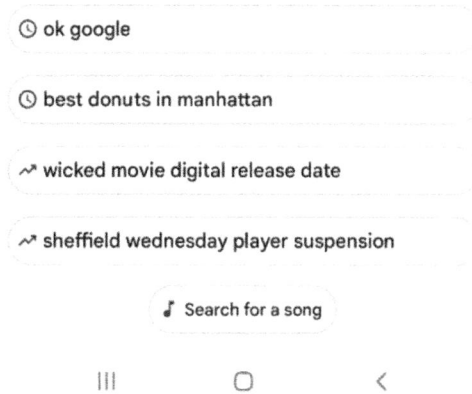

Figure 4-2. *Some examples of previous searches*

4. Say something starting with the words "OK Google…" – for
    example, I've used "OK Google, show me book shops in
    New York" (where Apress is based).

5. If all is well, we should see some results appear similar to those
    shown in Figure 4-3 and Figure 4-4, which show the search
    term used and the results, respectively.

Figure 4-3. *Google showing the search term we used
(highlighted in red)*

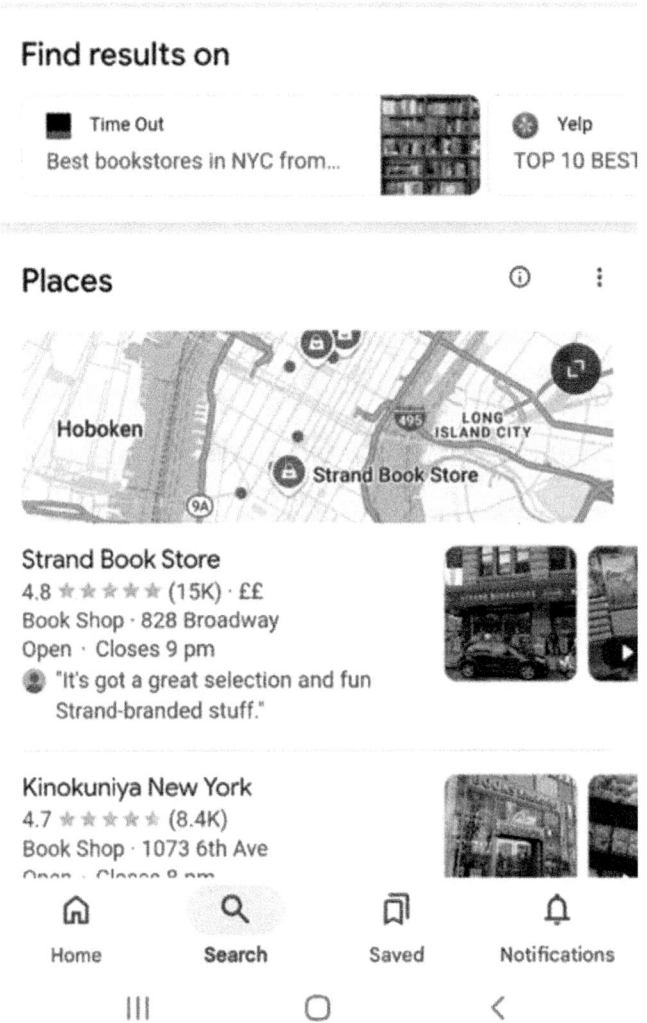

Figure 4-4. *Results of our voice search in Google*

See how easy it was to run the search? It might have taken a moment or two for the results to appear, but that doesn't matter – the key here is that we did it using our voice.

A survey by Adobe from a few years ago shows that the most popular search was for music, followed by the weather forecast and online searches – all of the reports show that these numbers are just going up, not down! It makes sense, given how easy it was to perform the search test we did just now; the challenge will be to replicate this on the web!

Okay, let's crack on: what would it look like if we were to add speech capabilities to our site? Let's dive in and take a look in more detail.

A Primer

Speech recognition as a technology is not that new – the principle dates back as far as the early 1950s, although more practical uses have only been around since the late 1980s.

When it comes to the web, adding speech capabilities is very straightforward – we can use the HTML5 Web Speech API, which is available in most browsers. The great thing about this API is that we only need our browser to get started, as the technology comes built-in to the likes of Chrome and Edge.

The exception is Firefox and IE – the CanIUse website (`https://caniuse.com/mdn-api_speechrecognition_lang`) shows both with minimal usage stats, so this shouldn't be an issue. However, I advise checking your analytics to verify if anyone uses either browser – I'll return to this later in this chapter.

The Speech API contains several interfaces that we can use to implement full speech capabilities; to implement speech recognition, we only need to use the SpeechRecognition API. (Another one that *could* be of interest is SpeechSynthesis, which throws up several challenges. I'll return to this later in the chapter.)

To learn more about the Speech Recognition API, head over to the main documentation at `https://developer.mozilla.org/en-US/docs/Web/API/SpeechRecognition`; I've also written a book about the API called Introducing the HTML5 Web Speech API, which is available from Apress.

There is a lot to consider when it comes to using the Speech Recognition interface – we'll explore some of the challenges shortly, but to start, let's work through a quick demo that shows how to implement the Speech Recognition API.

Creating a Basic Demo

Before we get into the nuts and bolts of our demo, there are a couple of assumptions I need to highlight:

- I've elected to create the demo run at the root of my C: drive; this is primarily for convenience, but please feel free to change the location if needed.

- You will need access to a microphone – I have a dedicated microphone with a stand, but you don't need anything fancy! If you have a headset with a microphone, this will work fine; a laptop with an in-built microphone will work just as well.

I've elected to create a new demo for this next exercise rather than use the previous one. It will show you what we need to add as a minimum and will not confuse it with changes from previous demos.

Okay, with that out of the way, let's get into our demo.

BASIC SPEECH TO TEXT

To assemble our primer demo, follow these steps:

1. First, we will create a new Next.js app – to do this, crack open a terminal prompt, then change the working folder to the C: drive. At the prompt, run this command, where `voice` will be the name of our demo project folder:

   ```
   npx create-next-app voice
   ```

2. You will likely see a prompt to install Next.js. If you do, press Y to accept it.

3. Once Next.js is downloaded, you will see a series of prompts (shown below) – press Enter to accept each default (shown in green):

   ```
   √ Would you like to use TypeScript? ... No / Yes
   √ Would you like to use ESLint? ... No / Yes
   √ Would you like to use Tailwind CSS? ... No / Yes
   √ Would you like your code inside a `src/` directory?
     ... No / Yes
   √ Would you like to use App Router? (recommended) ...
     No / Yes
   √ Would you like to use Turbopack for `next dev`? ...
     No / Yes
   √ Would you like to customize the import alias
     (`@/*` by default)? ... No / Yes
   ```

4. Node.js will then confirm that Next.js has been installed: at this point, open the project folder in your editor.

5. Once open, go ahead and create a new file, then add this code:

```
import { useEffect, useRef, useState } from "react";

const VoiceSearch = () => {
  ...INSERT DEFINITIONS HERE...
  return (
    ...INSERT CODE HERE...
  }
};

export default VoiceSearch;
```

6. Save the file as VoiceSearch.jsx in the \src\ components folder.

7. With a basic skeleton in place, we can flesh out our component with declarations. In the section marked "INSERT DEFINITIONS HERE", replace that line with these three definitions:

```
const [transcript, setTranscript] = useState("");
const [isListening, setIsListening] = useState(false);
const recognitionRef = useRef(null);
```

8. Next, we have three event handlers to add – for this, add a blank line after the last const recognitionRef... line, then add the first, called startListening:

```
const startListening = () => {
  if (!recognitionRef.current) {
    console.error(
      "SpeechRecognition instance is not available.
      Ensure your browser supports it."
    );
```

```
    return;
  }
  setIsListening(true);
  recognitionRef.current.start();

};
```

9. Leave a line blank after the end of the previous event handler, then add the second, which is called stopListening:

```
const stopListening = () => {
  if (!recognitionRef.current) {
    console.error(
      "SpeechRecognition instance is not available.
      Ensure your browser supports it."
    );
    return;
  }
  setIsListening(false);
  recognitionRef.current.stop();

};
```

10. For the third event handler, miss a line after the stopListening handler, then add this code:

```
const handleSearch = () => {
  // Simulate a search
  console.log("Searching for:", transcript);

};
```

11. To use them, we need to tell our component to initialize an instance of the Speech Recognition API as soon as the project runs – for this, leave a line blank after the previous event handler, then add this useEffect() block:

```
useEffect(() => {
    const SpeechRecognition =
      window.SpeechRecognition || window.
      webkitSpeechRecognition;
    if (!SpeechRecognition) {
      console.warn("SpeechRecognition is not supported
      in this browser.");
      return;
    }

    const recognition = new SpeechRecognition();
    recognition.continuous = true;
    recognition.interimResults = false;
    recognition.lang = "en-US";

    recognition.onresult = (event) => {
      const result = event.results[event.results.
      length - 1][0].transcript;
      setTranscript(result);
    };

    // Store the instance in the ref
    recognitionRef.current = recognition;

    // Cleanup on component unmount
    return () => {
      recognition.abort();
    };
  }, []);
```

12. With the event handlers and declarations in place, we can now turn our attention to the UI. For this, go ahead and add this code inside the return block (marked `"INSERT CODE HERE"`).

We have a fair bit of code to cover, so I will go through it in two parts – the first adds the opening lines for a container, followed by the Start Voice Search button:

```
<div
  style={{
    textAlign: "center",
    padding: "20px",
    fontFamily: "Arial, sans-serif",
  }}>
  <button
    onClick={startListening}
    disabled={isListening}
    style={{
      padding: "10px 20px",
      margin: "5px",
      backgroundColor: isListening ? "#ccc" :
      "#4CAF50",
      color: "white",
      border: "none",
      borderRadius: "5px",
      cursor: isListening ? "not-allowed" : "pointer",
      fontSize: "16px",
    }}>
    🎤 Start Voice Search
  </button>
```

13. The second part of the UI code covers a second button, this one stopping the Speech Recognition API when clicked:

```
    <button
      onClick={stopListening}
      disabled={!isListening}
      style={{
        padding: "10px 20px",
        margin: "5px",
        backgroundColor: !isListening ? "#ccc" :
        "#f44336",
        color: "white",
        border: "none",
        borderRadius: "5px",
        cursor: !isListening ? "not-allowed" :
        "pointer",
        fontSize: "16px",
      }}>
      ⏺ Stop
    </button>
    <p style={{ fontSize: "18px", marginTop: "20px",
    color: "#333" }}>
      <strong>Transcript:</strong> {transcript || "Say
      something..."}
    </p>
  </div>
);
```

14. Save the file. Next, go ahead and open page.js, then replace the entire contents with this code:

```
import VoiceSearch from "../components/VoiceSearch";
export default function Home() {
  return (
    <div
      style={{{
```

```
        width: "100dvw",
        height: "100dvh",
        display: "grid",
        placeItems: "center",
      }}
    >
        <h1>Voice Search React App</h1>
        <VoiceSearch />
    </div>
  );
```

15. Save the file, then close any files that are still open. Switch to a Node.js terminal session, then make sure the working folder is set to the demo folder. At the prompt, enter npm run dev and press Enter.

16. When prompted, browse to http://localhost:3000. If everything is running as expected, you should see the screen shown in Figure 4-5.

Voice Search React App

Transcript: Say something...

Search

Figure 4-5. Our primer demo for Voice Search

115

17. Try clicking Start Voice Search – you should see a prompt in your browser to enable the microphone: click Allow while using this application.

This step is a necessary security feature built into all browsers – on subsequent runs in the same session, it won't appear.

---

18. If all is well, we should see something akin to that shown in Figure 4-6 – this screenshot was taken from Chrome, but other browsers, such as Edge or Firefox, will look similar.

Figure 4-6. *Confirmation that the microphone is running*

19. Try saying something like "Hello" – the demo should pick up and display it on screen, where it says "Say something .... ." You will also see a confirmation of what is said if you open your browser's console log area, such as shown in Figure 4-7.

Download the React DevTools for a better develop

[Fast Refresh] rebuilding

[Fast Refresh] done in 1489ms

Searching for: hello

> |

Figure 4-7. *Faking the results of a search from the demo*

Phew – we've covered a lot, but this is only the start; we can do much more! This last demo has highlighted some useful features and points we should be aware of, so before we build a demo search example, let's first review the code changes we made in more detail.

Exploring the Code Changes

Adding voice capabilities can be a double-edged sword – the great thing about it is that it is very straightforward to implement; the downside is that we have to add a fair bit of code! There is one saving grace, though, which is that you will find yourself repeating a lot of what we add – it may not be precisely the same, but it will still cover the same events and functions as our demo.

So, what did we do? We began by creating a barebones Next.js project using the Next.js version of Create App – for our project, we chose default values that would be sufficient for our needs, but you may want to tweak these for your own projects. For the first change, we added a skeleton component file called VoiceSearch.jsx; we imported three packages from React and added the basic code for our component.

With the skeleton in place, we started to add the various event handlers for our component – we included handlers to control what happens when we start listening, stop listening, and perform the "search" (I'll come back to this one in a moment).

Although we do need event handlers, we also have to add the most essential part, which is initializing our instance of the API! Adding it requires a fair bit of code – we start with creating an instance of SpeechRecognition based on what is supported in your browser. We then added a check to ensure we can even use SpeechRecognition; if it is not supported, we drop out of the useEffect block. Next up, we created an instance of the API before adding several properties, which I've listed in Table 4-1.

Table 4-1. *SpeechRecognition API configuration properties used*

Property	Purpose
interimResults	This property controls whether we display results based on part searches. For example, if you type in "inte" (for "interim"), it would show results if it is set to true, which could be misleading! Set to false in our demo
continuous	We set this to true – this controls whether we show continuous results or a single one
lang	This property controls what language is set for the API – in this instance, we used US English but could have used any of several dozen languages! Note – if we do not set this property, it will return the language property set for the current browser user agent

For details of other properties, methods, and events available, please check the MDN documentation for the API at https://developer. mozilla.org/en-US/docs/Web/API/SpeechRecognition.

We can add other values, but these will depend on how you want to configure the API – for now, the ones we have are sufficient. To round out the useEffect, we added an onresult event handler, which trims the results of what is returned to just the text of the response (it returns other values, which are not needed). We then store this in state so we can use it again and stop the API, as we only need it running each time we search – running it all the time will pick up background speech, producing some odd results!

The last part of the code is the UI for our demo – this adds two buttons that start and stop the microphone based on when we want to use it. It also displays the results of what we say on screen when running the demo in the browser.

To finish things off, we ran a test of the `handleSearch` event handler, which displayed the results of what we searched for in the console.log area. Don't worry – this isn't something we would do in production: it's to show you how you can take the response from the transcript and do something with it later in your project! In our next demo, we'll look at how we could do a simple search later in this chapter.

Some Points to Note

Before we move on and turn this demo into a search component, there are a few things we should cover off, which will affect how you use the API:

- You will notice that although we used localhost, we should ideally run this in a secure environment under HTTPS – this will help encrypt anything passed in from the microphone to protect privacy and keep prying eyes (or should that be ears?) out. While the documentation at MDN doesn't specify that HTTPS is a must, given that most sites now use HTTPS by default, it makes sense to use it.

- Notice how we used `useEffect` blocks in this demo? This is key, as we need to control when the microphone is used – not only will it pick up any background chatter and potentially perform odd actions, but there is also the small matter of data privacy! For this reason, we need to limit when the microphone is available (and used) and not leave it to kick in by itself!

Okay, Let's move on: now that we've covered the basics of adding the Speech Recognition interface, let's take it up a step and turn our demo into a usable component.

Creating a Search Component

For our next demo, we will use the same code as the previous example but modify it to only show selected products in a list based on the voice input from the API.

The critical point here is that it is a simplified example intended to show how we *could* trigger a search – in reality, we'd make a few changes to develop this code into something more realistic! We'll come back to this shortly when we review the changes, but for now, let's take a look at how we can create our component in more detail.

As before, I'll create this as a new demo so that you can compare the changes we need to make between this and the previous primer demo.

CREATING A VOICE-DRIVEN SEARCH COMPONENT

To create our search component, follow these steps:

1. First, we will create a new Next.js app – to do this, crack open a terminal prompt, then change the working folder to the C: drive. At the prompt, run this command, where voice will be the name of our demo project folder:

```
npx create-next-app voice-search-demo
```

2. You will likely see a prompt to install Next.js. If you do, press Y to accept it.

3. Once Next.js is installed, you will see a series of prompts (shown below) – press Enter to accept each default (shown in green):

    √ Would you like to use TypeScript? ... No / Yes
    √ Would you like to use ESLint? ... No / Yes
    √ Would you like to use Tailwind CSS? ... No / Yes
    √ Would you like your code inside a `src/` directory?
        ... No / Yes
    √ Would you like to use App Router? (recommended) ...
        No / Yes
    √ Would you like to use Turbopack for `next dev`? ...
        No / Yes
    √ Would you like to customize the import alias (`@/*`
        by default)? ... No / Yes

4. Node.js will then confirm that Next.js is installed: at this point, open the project folder in your editor.

5. Once open, go ahead and create a new folder called components in the \src folder.

6. Next, open a new file, then add this code, which will act as the starting point for our component:

```
"use client";

import { useState, useEffect, useRef } from "react";

const products = [
  "Apple iPhone",
  "Apple MacBook",
  "Apple Watch",
  "Samsung Galaxy",
```

```
    "Samsung Notebook",
    "Samsung Tablet",
    "Google Pixel",
    "Google Nest",
  ];

  const SearchBar = () => {
    ...ENTER DECLARATIONS CODE HERE...
  return (
    ...ENTER UI CODE HERE...
    );
  };
```

7. Next, we need to add some declarations – for this, go ahead and add the following code to the head of the component:

```
const [query, setQuery] = useState("");
const [filteredProducts, setFilteredProducts] =
useState(products);
const [isListening, setIsListening] = useState(false);

const recognitionRef = useRef(null);

const startListening = () => {
  if (!recognitionRef.current) {
    console.error(
      "SpeechRecognition instance is not available.
      Ensure your browser supports it."
    );
    return;
  }
  setIsListening(true);
  recognitionRef.current.start();
};
```

8. We have a couple of useEffect() blocks we need to add to
    the head of the component – the first part defines an instance
    of the SpeechRecognition API:

```
useEffect(() => {
  const SpeechRecognition =
    window.SpeechRecognition || window.
    webkitSpeechRecognition;

  if (!SpeechRecognition) {
    console.warn("SpeechRecognition is not supported in
    this browser.");
    return;
  }

  const recognition = new SpeechRecognition();
  recognition.continuous = true;
  recognition.interimResults = false;
  recognition.lang = "en-US";
```

9. The second part defines some event handlers associated with
    the Speech Recognition API, which we need in place for the API
    to respond – at the same time, we add the closing brackets for
    the useEffect block:

```
recognition.onresult = (event) => {
  const transcript = event.results[0][0].transcript;
  setQuery(transcript);
  recognition.stop();
  setIsListening(false);

};
```

10. This handler takes care of any instance where the API
     generates an error:

```
recognition.onerror = (event) => {
  console.error("Error occurred in recognition:",
  event.error);
};
```

11. This event handler checks for when the API detects no more
     changes (i.e., the person has stopped talking):

```
recognition.onend = () => {
  recognition.stop();
  setIsListening(false);
};

// Store the instance in the ref
recognitionRef.current = recognition;

// Cleanup on component unmount
return () => {
  recognition.abort();
};
}, []);
```

12. The second useEffect block takes care of triggering the
     "search" process when query changes as a result of the API
     receiving a new value:

```
useEffect(() => {
  if (query === "") {
    setFilteredProducts(products);
  } else {
    setFilteredProducts(
      products.filter((product) =>
```

```
      product.toLowerCase().includes(query.to
      LowerCase())
    )
  );

  }
}, [query]);
```

13. With the declarations in place, let's turn our attention to the UI markup for our component – inside the `return()` block, add this code, starting with the opening for the component container:

```
<div
  style={{
    textAlign: "center",
    margin: "20px",
    fontFamily: "Arial, sans-serif",
  }}
>
    ...INSERT CODE HERE...
</div>
```

14. Next, add the component title and an input button inside the div, where indicated in the previous step:

```
<h1>Voice Search Product Demo</h1>
<input
  type="text"
  value={query}
  onChange={(e) => setQuery(e.target.value)}
  placeholder="Search for products..."
        style={{
    width: "300px",
```

```
            lineHeight: "20px",
            padding: "10px",
            borderRadius: "4px",
        }}
    />
```

15. For clarity, skip a line, then add this button code – this will
    enable the microphone, ready for use:

```
<button
    onClick={startListening}
    style={{
        padding: "10px 20px",
        margin: "10px 5px",
        backgroundColor: isListening ? "#ccc" : "#4CAF50",
        color: "white",
        border: "none",
        borderRadius: "5px",
        cursor: isListening ? "not-allowed" : "pointer",
        fontSize: "16px",
    }}
>
    {isListening ? "Listening..." : "🎤 Start Voice
    Search"}
</button>
```

16. We need some way to display the results – for this, add
    the following code to list the entries returned, along with a
    total number:

```
<div style={{ marginTop: "20px" }}>
  <h2>
    {filteredProducts.length == 1
      ? "1 result:"
      : `${filteredProducts.length} results:`}
  </h2>
  <ul>
    {filteredProducts.map((product, index) => (
      <li key={index}>{product}</li>
    ))}
  </ul>
</div>
</div>
```

17. Save the file as VoiceSearch.jsx in the \src\ components folder.

18. Next, go ahead and open page.js, then replace the entire contents with this code:

```
import SearchBar from "../components/SearchBar";

export default function Home() {
  return (
    <div>
      <link rel="icon" href="/favicon.ico" />
      <main>
        <SearchBar />
      </main>
    </div>
  );
}
```

19. Save the file, then close any files that are still open. Switch to a Node. js terminal session, then make sure the working folder is set to the demo folder. At the prompt, enter npm run dev and press Enter.

20. When prompted, browse to http://localhost:3000. If everything is running as expected, you should see the screen shown in Figure 4-8.

Voice Search Product Demo

Apple

Start Voice Search

3 results:
Apple iPhone
Apple MacBook
Apple Watch

Figure 4-8. *Results of searching using voice*

Oops – sorry – another lengthy demo! But, in my defense, I will say a lot of it is similar to the original primer, so this will help reinforce what we covered in the first demo. In reality, though, we only needed to make a few changes to get a basic search facility working. We can then develop it into something more akin to our needs and make it suitable for release into production. All in all, we've covered some useful changes in this last demo, so let's take a moment to review them in more detail.

Understanding What Changed

If you take a closer look at the code we created in this last demo, you'd be forgiven for thinking a sense of déjà vu; you've seen it somewhere before! Indeed, you have, as it formed the basis for our first demo, where I showed you how the Speech API works. There was a reason for reusing the code again – let me explain: it has a lot to do with reusability.

One of the great things about the API is that no matter where you use it, there will be instances where we need to write very similar code. So much so that it would make sense to convert it into modular functions we can drop straight into our environment! For now, though, I've left the code to help reinforce what we learned earlier. We can always come back and do that conversion at a later date.

All in all, we created a new barebones demo using the same default settings. The code itself is identical to the previous demo except for the following changes:

- I added a separate dummy data block so we had something to display; in an ideal world, we'd pass this in from an external data source (at least to the component). For now, though, what we have will suffice to show how it works.

- You will see that I've not included the handleSearch() function from the previous demo; instead, we're using a simple filter mechanism only to show those data entries that match the search parameters. In the same vein, the function is enough to show us how to make it work, but ideally, we'd want to move this to a separate component (particularly as we likely won't use the same filtering mechanism anyway!)

- I've also commented out the stopListening function; we need to be mindful of privacy and not keep the microphone active longer than required. Making this process manual means that we're relying on users shutting it off, which isn't likely to happen often – we can do this for them automatically after each search.

To round out the demo, we replaced the markup with a search box on the screen, plus a button and placeholder list. The button enables the microphone, while we used the placeholder to display the filtered results, depending on what is returned from our search function to the browser.

Okay, now that we've seen how to add basic speech recognition to our application, there is one point I do want to explore: what about text-to-speech? It's a good question – we've focused mainly on speech-to-text, as this is a core part of what we're trying to achieve with VSO. There are arguments for and against using text-to-speech in this instance, so let's look at some of them in more detail.

Should We Add Text-to-Speech Capabilities?

In the last two demos, we've focused on using speech-to-text recognition, as this is a recognized part of VSO. However, the Web Speech API includes APIs for both text-to-speech and speech-to-text – while there may be a natural inclination to use both, I'm not sure it would work. Let me explain.

Adding text-to-speech capabilities for searching means we would get auditory confirmation of the results returned from our search. It would *potentially* mean that anyone visually impaired could get some indication of what is returned and not feel excluded from using the website.

However – and this is where we need to step carefully – if we were to add text-to-speech recognition, then we would have to make sure the format of the results returned makes sense to someone who can't see them on screen. This format might be OK for a site that offers something like cookies (odd choice, but bear with me), but not so satisfactory if we're returning results from a search for something like hardware products.

The point here is that not only would we say how many results are returned, but we need to make them easily understood – something like cookies (such as "double choc chip cookies") would make sense, but not so for a product such as a "BS SYSTEMS PP Aluminium Coated Fixing Strap, 1.4m x" when spoken verbally!

It all comes down to what products or services you want to offer and whether you can make them available in an engaging format that makes sense to a visually impaired person. We don't want to exclude people unnecessarily, but we need to balance making this content available in the correct format against resources and costs.

This point brings us nicely into a super important stage – now that we've seen how to add speech recognition and get it to trigger a basic search, it's time for us to make some decisions. Implementing the feature at a technical level may be easy enough to do, but it will only be successful if we've considered all factors around how we will use it on our website. To help with this, I've listed some questions we can start with, so let's take a look at what we need to decide when using the API.

Making Some Decisions

Implementing the Speech Recognition API is technically easy, but as I've already mentioned, this is only part of the story – we need to decide how best to implement it **for our needs**.

It might seem a little odd that I've gone straight into building a demo first, but that was with good reason – speech recognition is still somewhat new, and to use it effectively, it's best to see a demo in action so we can understand how it works and where it can help us. With that in mind, let's take a look at some of the questions we need to ask ourselves (in no particular order):

- Offline access: it's important to note that some browsers talk directly to Google to process any requests and return the responses when using the API. As a result, you will find that the API can't be used offline in some cases. It's something we will need to bear in mind and factor into any design.

- Browser support may or may not be an issue: I touched on the fact that IE and Firefox do not support this API. While the former won't be an issue (as Edge is replacing it), the latter may be an issue for some: we will need to check our analytics to see what people are using. As a rough guideline, if it's below 1% of total usage, then you can decide if you want to include any changes (such as adding a banner to announce voice support) or work on the basis that Firefox gets the standard experience and other browsers receive the enhanced version.

- Feedback is another area we must explore: how would we display it? In our second demo, for example, we displayed a list of results – but what if we didn't have any? I put in a rudimentary count, but this seems a little impersonal; would a message along the lines of "Sorry, we don't have any results" work better?

- When searching for an item, we must consider what sort of input mechanism would work best: a drop-down box or a regular input field. Using the former might be appropriate if we were maintaining a history list of entries (as you will see on Google), but if we were using voice, would this be as effective, or would a standard input box work better?

- Language support: as websites are available in any country (save for where access may be blocked in a particular country), we should consider whether we want to offer support in different languages. While the Speech API can offer support in multiple languages, we need to make sure that our data ties in with the chosen language(s); it would be wise to ensure we comply with any privacy concerns that could be raised in those countries, as well as make sure we have the right content for each country!

Just a few things to think about! We should remember that we don't have to implement everything immediately, so a part of this process might also include questions about what we want to support now or in the longer term. A good example of this would be languages – we might want to support more than just English, but adding it could be a gradual process. We might include Dutch, for example (if we were in Holland, where they speak both), but other languages would come at a later date.

Extending the Support

Okay, enough questions: let's move on to something different.

You may remember from Chapter 3 that one of the tactics we can use when optimizing for voice search is to add a frequently asked question (or FAQ) page on our site. Some people might consider this unnecessary, but when used with other SEO tactics, it can help keep your site relevant and improve its ranking.

As part of this, I talked about using a relatively new feature called the Speakable structured data – in essence, we mark a specific part of the site as the tin says, "speakable." Let me explain what I mean by this with an example.

Let's say you ask Google by voice what the latest news is on the New York Times website – if it determines the content that it finds meets the standard, then it will respond with something appropriate (it might be something like wildfires in a state, latest on US elections …. You get the idea!).

The best way to look at this option is that it is very similar to the featured snippets trick we discussed earlier – we pick out a chunk of information that answers a query; the speakable data does the same thing but vocally, not on screen.

So, why would we use it? The answer is simple – it's all about increasing our SEO ranking: the speakable structured data is just one way to optimize our site. Although we can't guarantee that Google will choose content from our site, it is still a free option – at least because we don't have to pay for a service!

The only actual costs are those of implementing it – we can do this either in a limited beta testing or once it becomes an officially stable version. There are some limitations we need to consider when it comes to implementing this data though, so let's take a look through and see what we have to bear in mind when adding the data block.

Limitations of Using Speakable

Implementing the speakable structured data block may be easy from a technical perspective, but it's a whole different kettle of fish when it comes to the *practicalities* of using it! The feature is still in beta at the time of writing, so there may well be changes coming – in the meantime, there are a few limitations we should be aware of:

- The feature is still in beta, so we must thoroughly test any implementation that uses it **if** you decide to go with it. It might be more prudent to defer until a later stage!

- Speakable is only available in English at present, but there are plans to support more languages over time.

- At the time of writing, speakable is only available on Google devices; it's suited (at present) to news articles, but there is scope to expand this to cover more content types.

- We can test speakable with Google's Rich Results Tester
  at `https://search.google.com/test/rich-results`,
  but only if hosted on a publicly accessible domain (it
  does not work using localhost).

- When answering, Google uses an algorithm to
  determine if the selected answer is relevant; details of
  what this looks like are not available, so there is no way
  to know if your content is good enough to be selected.

- We must ensure our content is relevant, factually
  correct, and clear. These checks will help meet the
  criteria for selection, but it does not automatically
  mean that Google will select content from our site!

Please note – these limitations are present at the time of writing;
things may change in the future as speakable transitions from beta
to a stable production version. If you would like to learn more, then
please head over to the documentation for speakable, hosted at
this link: `https://developers.google.com/search/docs/appearance/structured-data/speakable`

With all of that in mind, I will take you through using it, but only as a
walkthrough – we'll use the voice-search-demo site (running under Next.
js version 15) we created in a previous demo so I can show you what to
expect when it comes to updating your own code.

WALKTHROUGH – IMPLEMENTING THE SPEAKABLE SPECIFICATION

For this walkthrough, I will use the voice-search-demo demo that we created earlier – to set the speakable structured data content for our site, follow these steps:

1. First, crack open the `page.js` file at the root of the `/src` folder, then add this import immediately below the one for the SearchBar component:

```
import Script from "next/script";
```

2. Next, leave a line blank, then add this constant, which defines some values for the <head> element of the page:

```
export const metadata = {
  title: "Voice Search Component Demo",
  name: "description",
  content: "A demo for voice controlled search using
  Next.js.",
};
```

3. Scroll down a bit to the `Home()` function, then add this constant declaration immediately before the `return()` statement:

```
const speakableMarkup = {
  "@context": "https://schema.org",
  "@type": "Article",
  name: "Speakable Structured Data Demo",
  description:
    "This is a demo article showing the implementation
    of speakable structured data in Next.js.",
          speakable: {
              "@type": "SpeakableSpecification",
```

```
        xpath: ["/html/body/div[1]/main/h1",
        "/html/body/div[1]/main/p[1]"],
      },
};
```

4. We're almost done with the changes – the last one is to add this block of markup immediately below the call to `<SearchBar />` and before the closing `</div>` tag:

```
<h1>Speakable Structured Data Demo</h1>
 <p>
   This is a simple demo of implementing speakable
   structured data in a Next.js 15 application.
 </p>
 <p>
   The content here can be marked up for voice
   assistants to read
   aloud.
 </p>
</main>
<Script
  id="speakable-script"
  type="application/ld+json"
  dangerouslySetInnerHTML={{ __html: JSON.
  stringify(speakableMarkup) }}
/>
```

5. Save and close all files.

If we were doing this for real, we would test the code from the domain you used (assuming it's not localhost, as outlined earlier). We can potentially also do this using Google's Rich Results Test facility, although I didn't get any sensible results when trying with the "paste code" option!

Nonetheless, there are some valuable points I want to go through, so let's quickly review the code changes before moving on to our next task.

As an aside, you might recognize some of the code used in this demo – it's lifted from Chapter 3, where we added standard Structured Data, which uses the same format.

Breaking Apart the Code Changes

Implementing the Speakable tag in Next.js highlights an interesting conundrum. Although we only need to make a couple of changes, one requires using a tag that could be dangerous if not used correctly! Let's look at the code we worked through in more detail to understand what I mean.

The first step in the last demo was to import the `Script` component from Next.js – we then added a constant that defines some metadata that we would typically see in the `<head>` block on a page. If you looked further down, you would expect to see a `<head>` tag for this or something similar – as this is now supported natively in Next.js 15, we don't need to use `next/head` or manually inject `<head>` – this is done for us automatically, using the metadata block we specified in the code.

Next, we created the `speakableMarkup` const, which contains all the values required for the speakable structured tag. This const includes entries such as `@context`, `@type,` and `name`; the entry of real interest is under speakable. Here, we set the tag type, plus the xPath (or route to) the tags we want to have spoken if called for by Google. In this case, the `xPath` refers to the `H1` and `p` tags in the body of our UI. We round things out by updating the UI for our page – the main change is to add the speakable block at the end using the Script component.

This is where things get interesting – implementing this code highlights a few points we must consider when using the tag. Before I go through these, let's take a quick look at an explanation for the three tags we've specified:

1. JSON-LD Markup

   - Defines the structured data with @context set to https://schema.org

   - Specifies the @type as NewsArticle

   - Includes the speakable property with a SpeakableSpecification object pointing to specific sections (cssSelector) of the page

2. HTML Elements

   - The <div> and <p> elements are identified as speakable content using their CSS selectors.

3. Use Case

   - This example assumes you're marking up a news article, but it can be adapted for other content types supported by the Speakable schema.

The first point I want to highlight is that while we've specified the elements that should be speakable, we would typically hide this markup on the page and only present it in the markup.

We've not specified CSS in our demo, so we'd need to correct this if we develop this code into production.

The real danger point here is that we have to use a specific tag – dangerouslysetInnerHTML – which is known to present a level of risk. Using it isn't ideal, as it does expose us to XSS attacks if we're not careful! That said, the speakable element is still in beta, so there is scope for the Next development team to work out an option that fits in better with the metadata tag and doesn't require us to use the `dangerouslysetInnerHTML` tag in our codebase.

Okay, let's move on: so far, our focus has been on desktop devices, even though we have touched on using mobiles in several places! (Remember the voice test we did at the start of the chapter, anyone?)

While this has worked so far, it would be very remiss of us not to consider mobile support – what would that look like? It's an interesting question, and the answer might be more straightforward or complicated than you think.

Adapting for Mobile Devices

Mmm, interesting end to that last section, I think! There is a good reason for that statement, so let me explain.

The Web Speech API we are using has been supported in most browsers, at least for the last few years – this handily includes both desktop and mobile! It means that from a technical perspective, we shouldn't need to do too much to get it working on either platform.

That said, there will be some changes we need to make, but more to *how* we use it. Let's have a look at some of the areas we need to investigate:

- On desktop, we need to grant permissions for the browser to use a microphone; while mobile devices will have an inbuilt microphone, this should be accessible in our browser, but the steps for enabling it will be different. In our demo, I created a button for this purpose. For example, there is already a microphone button on tablets, so it would be better to see if we can use it instead of a dedicated button.

- For those developing for Android or iOS, we can still use Next.js but will have to use a tool such as

Capacitor to translate Next.js code into its native-ready equivalent. This *might* throw constraints up that means we need to use an alternative – it's something we would need to investigate.

- Space may be an issue: for desktop, we can add and display the relevant buttons and icons we need to control the API, but we may need to know how these appear on a mobile device. We might be tempted to automatically auto-enable cell phones for VSO, but this could (and likely would) lead to privacy concerns and would not be recommended. Instead, we could hide them in a slide-in menu or equivalent, as long as they are clear and we can get at them quickly.

- The UI: given that mobile devices don't have the same amount of space as desktops, what should we do to ensure that mobile users still have as good an experience as desktop users? Do mobile users need access to all of the same features or just a subset? Are there any hardware differences we must be mindful of that could make the mobile implementation easier or harder? Will it be the same for both iOS and Android users, or will there be differences between both and desktop?

This is just a few pointers to get us started – the best recommendation I can give is to build a mockup and try it out! Yes, I know it might seem obvious, but this is still a relatively new technology, and it will take time for people to get accustomed to it. At the same time, this would be a perfect candidate for testing in a focus group environment or even through A/B experimentation.

Okay, time to move on: we've covered a lot of points throughout this chapter, but before we explore adding support for internationalization in VSO, I want to explore one final topic, which is to answer this question.

How Can We Improve the Experience?

It might seem a little odd to start this section with a question, but it's super critical to VSO's success! Let me explain.

From experience over the years, I've often seen people implement new tools or features (not just on websites, but generally) – they may work in the short term but often end up dying a slow death as the processes to support those features or tools do not exist. It's the same with buying a new car: you wouldn't sell it without some form of after-sales service, would you?

I know the after-sales process isn't as glamorous as making the initial purchase (so to speak), but the post-implementation care is just as critical! To help with this, I've put together some ideas as a starting point for conversations – let's have a look:

- The most important one is research, research, research. I know I've said that three times, but it's super critical: you need to know what your competitors are doing, who is using VSO, if customers are clamoring for an update, if your markets are changing, and so on. How you might implement changes is down to individual circumstances, but we should at least be on top of what to change! You might also find that companies are willing to share some details as a collaboration on best practices – this will be worth its weight in gold and not something we should ignore.

- An interesting point – would geolocation make a difference? I've seen many instances where Google advertises something like "cookie shops near me" – we could use the same principle on our sites. We'd need something like the Geolocation API that's available in browsers to pinpoint where the customer is, but it shouldn't be too difficult to work out where a local branch, store, or outfit of our company is for the customer, based on their query.

A good starting point for this API will be the documentation on MDN – you can get to it at `https://developer.mozilla.org/en-US/docs/Web/API/Geolocation_API/Using_the_Geolocation_API`.

- Dialects and languages always need checking and refining. If you happen to live in a region where dialects could be an issue, then it's worth checking the Speech APIs to see if there might be a better option to use that customers prefer. The same applies to languages – the Speech API supports a lot of languages, so over time, we may want to add a new one (but don't forget: we need to add content, labels, and so on – I'll come back to this in Chapter 5, where we look at internationalization).

- One essential point is to focus on what customers say: if there is a spike on, say, "veg delivered near to me," then make sure this is picked up and ranked higher/made more visible in the search results.

- It's worth researching keywords being used to monitor for any changes we need: these change over time, so we need to be on top of this and make any changes as needed. This is why it's essential to do as much as we can to make it easier for non-technical people to edit content, cutting out the need for code releases (and required time).

- One of the best ways to improve it is not to make changes but to have champions around the company! Having them in place will depend on what your company does and the resources available, but why not have someone (or a small team) advocate the benefits of using this new feature and helping others get accustomed to it? It's a brilliant way to get feedback, even if it is only anecdotal! This person could also be responsible for disseminating any changes needed to the relevant teams around the company so they are prioritized and not lost in the ether.

These are just a few things to think about – I'm sure you will come up with more! The key is to ensure that we have processes to create the feature and manage, refine, and develop it once we release it into production.

Okay, let's crack on: we come to one of my favorite questions and one that is related to what we've just been talking about – how do we take things further? It's a great question – let's crack it open and see what we could do to extend and develop our solution.

Taking It Further

Over the last few pages, we've covered a lot of detail about the Web Speech API and, more specifically, the Speech Recognition interface (or API). We've seen that it's important to keep maintaining and developing content for it, such as analyzing what people ask and adding top answers as FAQs on the site. However, there is more we could do – particularly to take it up a level: what about that subject that everyone is talking about, AI?

Well, strange as it may seem, AI could help us further develop the experience for our customers. It might raise some questions about subjects like privacy, but if we put them aside for now, let's look at three example areas that could be worth pursuing to help elevate our use of VSO. We'll begin with tokenizing our input – a strange subject, but you'll soon see why this can help us!

Tokenizing the Input

One of the challenges we will face when implementing VSO is ensuring that what we receive as input is indeed what the user said – after all, words like "three" and "tree" can sound very similar, depending on the accent and clarity of input!

There is something we can do to help mitigate this, though, which is called tokenizing. Don't worry; this isn't a security subject, but it's more about breaking down what is said into single words. How does this help us?

Well, it all boils down to recognition – when using VSO, we're encouraged to use long-tail terms such as "The quick brown fox jumps over the lazy dog." Said normally, it would sound fine, but the browser may not be able to interpret as well if it doesn't break it down into single units of words, or, in this case, tokens (hence the name).

Let's take that example and add it to some demo code you can run:

```
const natural = require('natural');

console.log(natural.PorterStemmer.tokenizeAndStem(
  "The quick brown fox jumps over the lazy dog."
  )
)
```

If we were to run this in a site, we would get back the following output:

```
[ 'The',
  'quick',
  'brown',
  'fox',
  'jumps',
  'over',
  'the',
  'lazy',
  'dog' ]
```

It might seem a little cumbersome, but here's the rub – not only does it help the machine understand where there are spaces (and consequently each word), but it could potentially recognize key words or numbers and act on them accordingly.

For example, if it detects a particular phrase, such as "switch to French language," it could change the default language on the Speech API to support French. It might also detect if we included a number in the query – this might be to return a set of results limited to the number, if your visitor asked for the top five restaurants in your local area. Okay, granted, these examples are a little contrived, but hopefully, you get where we're going with it!

As an aside, it might be worth exploring the Hamming technique, which we can use to measure the similarity between two spoken phrases. This will help determine whether we should add something to an FAQ page – people might ask variants of a question, but the basic premise of the question is the same, so the more they ask, the more likely it should be on that page! If you would like to learn more, there is a helpful article on the BlogRocket website at `https://blog.logrocket.com/natural-language-processing-node-js/#what-natural-language-processing`.

Assessing the Impact of AI

We've covered a lot of content on using the HTML Web Speech API, but there is one area we should explore – and one that some people might call the "elephant in the room," as it can be a little controversial! That topic is the use of AI – let me explain what I mean.

Chatbots. Love or hate them, they are becoming more prevalent each year – websites see them as an easy way to help answer simple questions and relieve the pressure on staff to focus on more complex queries.

While this can work well, I've seen (from experience) that many don't work as well as they should and that the older generation of customers frequently prefer having a voice-to-voice conversation and not having to type something into a website. Chatbots are, by default, usually only able to answer simple queries – anything more complex will often end up sending them into a spin!

While researching this book, it gave me something to think about: what if we could do something different, combine the HTML Web Speech API with AI, and create an *atypical* chatbot? Yes, you read correctly – an atypical chatbot. Having such a chatbot might seem odd, but let me explain what I mean in more detail, beginning with some background to my idea.

AI can play a broader role in optimizing content for voice search – for some inspiration, take a look at the article by Valentina Izzo, available at `https://wordlift.io/blog/en/ai-optimized-voice-search-content/`.

Background

One of the downsides of a chatbot is that it only works based on how we program it – it means that it can typically only handle simple queries. These are likely to fail if they can't pick out specific details needed to respond, resulting in irritated customers, who will see it as a poor excuse to save money and not provide excellent service.

Instead, why not combine AI and the Web Speech API to create a more intelligent chatbot? Let's take a look at how we could build something as part of the next demo – I'll strip it back to the core for now, but hopefully, it will give you a flavor of what is possible when combining the two APIs.

A Possible Answer

For this next demo, we will do something different – as this hooks into AI, I've thought, "Why not get AI to provide a possible answer for us?" It might sound a wild idea, but bear with me on this.

Over the last few years, there has been an increasing trend to use AI to help code features – it's a more efficient use of time and resources. If people have already built something similar, why not leverage that ability rather than reinvent the wheel? Sure, AI is not 100% infallible and can make mistakes, but if we can get a large chunk of the work done quicker, it's worth spending time doing it! With this in mind, I asked ChatGPT to create some code using this prompt.

> *Create a Next.js version 15 proof of concept application of a simple chatbot, as follows: - Use the HTML5 Web Speech API to recognize text and convert it into speech - Use OpenAI to provide a search service - Add an example prompt that could point to a dummy FAQ page link - All responses should be as human as possible.*

I then added some tweaks to the code to fill in some gaps – the final answer forms the basis for our next demo.

Note – I've deliberately not tested this answer, so I can't vouch for how it works; the aim was more for using AI to get us started and see what it could produce if we take this further in a real-world scenario.

USING AI FOR VOICE INPUT

Before we get stuck into the code, there are a couple of things to note:

- ChatGPT generated this code to work on Next.js version 15.

- If we were to build this, we would need a key from OpenAI to access their API.

Okay, let's dig into the code and see what we could build:

- We'd need a Next.js 15 application as the basis for our code – if you're using an earlier version (say 14 or even 13), it *should* work, but the unknown factor will be OpenAI and what versions their plugin will support.

- I'm assuming for this walkthrough that we'd have a working Next.js application (ideally at version 15, but 13 or 14 will do) and that we'd install the OpenAI npm package using the traditional method of `npm install openai`.

- For OpenAI, we'd need an API key but also need to discuss with OpenAI to work out the costs of using it at an enterprise level. A good starting point would be to view what OpenAI offers at `https://openai.com/chatgpt/enterprise/` – OpenAI doesn't offer explicit pricing for this level, so we'd need to work out what we'd need and negotiate a reasonable cost.

This will also tie into what we would use internally, as well as which browsers we support, etc. It might be more practical to support only a small set of browser users to assess ROI before expanding to a broader audience.

Digging into the code, we could add something like this:

1. The first part is a configuration change, which identifies issues such as unsafe life cycles or legacy APIs. This setting has been active by default from Next.js 13.5.1, so it is only really necessary for pages:

```
// next.config.js
module.exports = {
  reactStrictMode: true,
};
```

2. This next part forms the core of the code/project — we create the SpeechRecognition component. It may not look the same as other examples we created earlier in this chapter, but you should still see some similarities. We start with defining some constants, as well as the instance of the SpeechRecognition API:

```
// components/SpeechRecognition.js
import { useState } from 'react';
const SpeechRecognition = ({ onTextRecognized }) => {
  const [isListening, setIsListening] =
  useState(false);
  const [recognizedText, setRecognizedText] =
  useState('');
```

```
const startListening = () => {
  if (!('webkitSpeechRecognition' in window)) {
    alert('Web Speech API is not supported in this
    browser.');
    return;
  }

  const recognition = new webkitSpeechRecognition();
  recognition.lang = 'en-US';
  recognition.continuous = false;
  recognition.interimResults = false;

  recognition.onstart = () => {
    setIsListening(true);
  };
```

3. The next part covers some of the event handlers we need for
    SpeechRecognition to operate – where we have three: one for
    when SpeechRecognition finishes successfully, one if there is
    an error, and the other if SpeechRecognition is stopped:

```
recognition.onresult = (event) => {
  const text = event.results[0][0].transcript;
  setRecognizedText(text);
  if (onTextRecognized) {
    onTextRecognized(text);
  }
};

recognition.onerror = (event) => {
  console.error('Speech recognition error:',
  event.error);
};
```

```
recognition.onend = () => {
  setIsListening(false);
};

recognition.start();
};
```

4. The second half covers the display of the results of the API –
    anything we say into our microphone will be rendered in
    this markup:

```
return (
  <div>
    <button onClick={startListening}
    disabled={isListening}>
      {isListening? 'Listening...' : 'Start Listening'}
    </button>
    <p>Recognized Text: {recognizedText}</p>
  </div>
);

};

export default SpeechRecognition;
```

5. We then move to the next component – this displays a response
    from our chatbot, which we tie into OpenAI, and import into
    what will be the main page for this demo (or whichever page
    you decide to use):

```
// components/ChatResponse.js
import { useState } from 'react';

const ChatResponse = ({ prompt }) => {
  const [response, setResponse] = useState('');
```

```
const fetchResponse = async () => {
  try {
    const res = await fetch('/api/chat', {
      method: 'POST',
      headers: { 'Content-Type': 'application/
      json' },

      body: JSON.stringify({ prompt }),
    });
    const data = await res.json();
    setResponse(data.response);
  } catch (error) {
    console.error('Error fetching response:', error);
  }
};

return (
  <div>
    <button onClick={fetchResponse}>Get Response
    </button>
    <p>Chatbot Response: {response}</p>
  </div>
);

};

export default ChatResponse;
```

6. To help build out the basics of our demo, I asked ChatGPT to create some dummy pages – the intention being that if we asked a question such as "Where could we find answers to common questions?" it would point us to the FAQ page, with a link for us to click:

```
// pages/api/chat.js
import { Configuration, OpenAIApi } from 'openai';
const configuration = new Configuration({
  apiKey: process.env.OPENAI_API_KEY,
});

const openai = new OpenAIApi(configuration);

export default async function handler(req, res) {
  if (req.method === 'POST') {
    const { prompt } = req.body;

    try {
      let response;
      if (prompt.toLowerCase().includes('faq')) {
        response = 'You can find answers to common
        questions on our FAQ page here: [FAQ Page]
        (http://localhost:3000/faq).';
      } else {
        const completion = await openai.
        createCompletion({
          model: 'text-davinci-003',
          prompt,
          max_tokens: 150,
        });
        response = completion.data.choices[0].
        text.trim();
      }
      res.status(200).json({ response });
    } catch (error) {
      console.error('OpenAI API error:', error);
      res.status(500).json({ error: 'Failed to fetch
      response from OpenAI' });
    }
```

```
  } else {
    res.setHeader('Allow', ['POST']);
    res.status(405).end(`Method ${req.method} Not
    Allowed`);
  }
}
```

7. I've touched on the pages I asked ChatGPT to create – here's
    the second, which is the FAQ page:

```
// pages/faq.js
export default function FAQ() {
  return (
    <div>
      <h1>FAQ Page</h1>
      <section id="general">
        <h2>General Questions</h2>
        <p>Here are answers to common questions about
        our service.</p>
      </section>
      <section id="technical">
        <h2>Technical Support</h2>
        <p>Find technical support details and
        troubleshooting tips.</p>
      </section>
    </div>
  );
}
```

8. To tie everything together, we'd need to import the
    ChatResponse component into our home page (or selected
    page, if different), and set it to display text when it received
    input from the API:

```
// pages/index.js
import { useState } from 'react';
import SpeechRecognition from '../components/
SpeechRecognition';
import ChatResponse from '../components/ChatResponse';

export default function Home() {
  const [prompt, setPrompt] = useState('');
  const handleTextRecognized = (text) => {
    console.log('Recognized text:', text);
    setPrompt(text);
  };
  return (
    <div>
      <h1>Chatbot with Web Speech API</h1>
      <SpeechRecognition onTextRecognized={handleText
      Recognized} />
      <ChatResponse prompt={prompt} />
    </div>
  );
}
```

9. At this point, we'd save everything and then run it in a development server to see what it does and if it needs further tweaking.

Mmm, even though we've not run it fully, I suspect this could be the start of something interesting! I know some people might be scared about the impact of AI (and that's true, it's starting to have a real impact everywhere), but one can't ignore that elephant: AI is here to stay, and it's time to embrace it so we can see what it could do for us now and in the future.

Understanding the Rationale and Limitations

At the start of this section, I mentioned that implementing chatbots, particularly those with AI, can be a bit of a double-edged sword. I think this deserves a little explanation, as I am sure some of you will think this comment is controversial! Let me explain what I mean.

Over the years, I've seen many companies implement chatbots to varying degrees; I often have to use them when getting hold of specific companies who don't believe in providing decent old-fashioned telephone support! However, nine times out of 10, I don't always see chatbots being implemented that well – it might be a dedicated one or one done based on using WhatsApp, but it doesn't matter; I still see areas where they could use more work to make them easier to navigate, slicker, and easier to escape if things go wrong.

Chatbots can perform a practical task, but they need to be tested thoroughly and put in front of people who will use them before releasing them into the wild. So, with this in mind, I've put together a few points to consider around why chatbots can be great to implement, plus some limitations that we need to bear in mind, particularly when using AI:

- The most crucial point to remember is that this technology is still relatively new – it will take time for people to get used to interacting with it. Implemented correctly, it will bring us closer to imitating what we would do if we were interacting with a human, but this will take time to achieve.

- From experience, companies have implemented chatbots with great intentions, but I am not convinced they align the experience with their target markets! Chatbots are aimed more at a younger generation or those who are (shall we say) more "computer-aware" than others. A standard chatbot needs to be programmed very carefully to get it right – the advantage of tying AI in gives it a more natural feel, as AI can better interpret what the customer wants, rather than relying on preprogramming responses that are not always as natural as they should be.

- The downside of using AI is that you may find content leaking in from other sites outside of your own, if the aim is only to search your site; there is no guarantee this will be accurate! While it might be helpful in some instances to have this content come in from other sources, we need to bear in mind the risk that it may be inaccurate, outdated, or, worse still, defamatory – all of which will reflect poorly on your site's reputation!

- Chatbots were only ever designed to complete relatively simple tasks. With AI, this could potentially up the game, but we still need to be mindful of something: AI should not be an excuse for taking over good customer support.

- Implementing AI in voice search will help extend the experience to less able people and make them feel as much a part of the same experience that able-bodied people get. The issue is that voice search won't necessarily work for everyone; we have to be selective about what we can implement to get the biggest "bang for buck" (i.e., the most significant impact with the available resources).

Ooh, just a few things to think about! I can see that chatbots will play an increasing role in supporting customers in the future. Still, we must ensure they are thoroughly tested and operate as expected before we release them for general use by the broader customer base.

If you want to take things even further, look at `https://chat-with-siri.vercel.app/chat`. This site is a demo I found while researching this book, which hooks into using Siri for searching websites!

Summary

Wow, that was one meaty chapter! Adding voice capabilities to your site opens up a world of possibilities, as long as it's done right and we maintain it continuously. We've covered a lot of content through this chapter, so let's take a moment to review what we have learned.

We started way back when (yes, it seems a long time ago!) with a basic primer on using the Web Speech API, specifically the SpeechRecognition interface. We then worked on converting the code into a usable component – we saw that given the code used in the primer, we did not have to make too many changes to get a starting solution to work!

Next came the point where we need to make some decisions about how we implement the API – granted it seems a little backward to do this after the demo, but this will give you some background to work on when making the decisions. We then switched to exploring some ideas for extending, improving (and developing) the experience further and making allowances for what we would need to do to support mobile devices.

To round out the chapter, we then stepped things up a little and explored a few ideas for really developing our solution further – we touched on two topics in particular, namely, how to understand the content more accurately as well as using AI to give our solution more power and take it to the next level.

Okay, on that note, we've reached the end of the chapter; we still have more to cover! For the last part of this journey, we're going international to explore how to add new language support when using VSO. The question is, though, "Ben je klaar om met mij mee te doen?" or "Are you ready to join me?"

CHAPTER 5

Going International

So far, we've focused on the key areas that can affect voice-driven SEO, but one thing is still missing – what about international support?

It may be OK if your website is only used by people able to speak, say, English, but that may not always be the case; what should we do about anyone visiting who doesn't speak our language of choice?

For this chapter, we'll look at how we can add support for other languages and what to consider to maintain voice SEO for our site. To begin with, let's first work on what we need to investigate so we can put together a strategy plan for adding the extra voice support.

Identifying Areas to Target

So – where do we start?

It is a great question – this is potentially one of those areas where we could get sucked into the proverbial rabbit hole if we're not careful!

For a task like this, I would recommend a whiteboarding session within your team, where we leave nothing off the table; there is a lot to consider, and a lot will depend on how your current site is set up. To help as a starting point, here are a few areas to consider – not in any particular order, and with no focus on what the answer should be (yet):

- Languages: choice, detection, folder structure.

- Accuracy.

© Alex Libby 2025
A. Libby, *Beginning Voice Search Optimization*, Design Thinking,
https://doi.org/10.1007/979-8-8688-1841-7_5

- Cultural differences.

- Creating a roadmap.

- Data: where will it come from, and how will we store or access it?

- SEO: how do our choices affect it? Are they limited, or can we choose?

- Responsibilities: we need to maintain this, so can we build processes to manage it?

- Visual UI changes, mainly where there may be cultural differences (e.g., right-to-left, for Arabic).

- Testing: both unit and integration/acceptance testing need to be covered.

Just a few things to think about! Some of what you come up with will have reasonably obvious answers, such as storing labels if you already have a working data source present. Others will be less obvious or require more discussion of issues that could complicate matters pop up!

Assuming you have developed some workable ideas, the next stage will be to put these in order. I've put together an example for you to indicate what kind of priority each item should have – this should hopefully give you an idea of what to expect. Let's take a look at each stage in more detail, beginning with the essentials.

Prioritizing Changes

Let's assume we've come up with a few ideas about what we need to tackle – it doesn't matter if it's technical or not; every idea counts! While working out what we need to tackle should come pretty quickly, the more challenging part is figuring out the details – let me explain why.

One of the challenges we face will be the site structure – for some of you, this won't be an issue if you are working on implementing language support in a greenfield project. However, I think many of you may have to implement it on an existing site, either soon after the initial launch or one that has a degree of maturity.

This constraint could be an issue because we may have to reconfigure how we host pages to support new locales. Let's take, for example, the Next. js website we created back in Chapter 3 – I set this up to use the new App Router structure. If we wanted to add English locale support, all we do is add a new /en folder at the root of the /app folder – Next will pick this up and treat it as if we were browsing to `http://localhost:3000/en`. The same applies to French support – this would be /fr for `http://localhost:3000/fr`, or how about /it for Italian support at `http://localhost:3000/it`? You get the idea!

However, if we're not using the App Router option or using something like standard React, our site may not be set up to support this, and we may need to add routing manually to support the same locale. That's why we must first get the basics in place for English (or your local language) before we even consider adding other languages!

Okay, enough of that doom: let's work through that example prioritization I mentioned earlier to see how things may hang together.

The Checklist

I've written this next part as a form of checklist, as the reality is that we'll need to check tasks off once we complete them. I've split them into three groups:

- Group 1: Foundation

- Group 2: Enhancing User Experience and Performance

- Group 3: Advanced Features and Compliance

Let's look at these in turn, starting with Group 1, Foundation.

Phase 1: Foundation

This phase takes care of the critical essentials to get us off the ground – we have to start with whatever your local language is, then follow it with any other languages you want to support. I've outlined specific areas and tasks to explore in Table 5-1.

Table 5-1. *The Foundation task list*

Area	Task(s)
Language Strategy and Structure	Define URL structure (/en/, /fr/, /es/). Implement next-intl for translations. Set up automatic/manual language detection (browser settings, URL path, flag switcher)
Content Management and Accuracy	Store translations in JSON or a CMS for easier updates Define a process to maintain translation consistency
Basic SEO and Voice Search Setup	Add hreflang tags for multilingual SEO Ensure metadata (title, description, alt text) is translated Implement structured data (Schema.org) to improve voice search results
Speech API and Basic VSO Integration	Detect and transcribe voice input (speech-to-text) Optimize for question-based queries ("Where can I find X?") Ensure the search query respects the current language setting

Phase 2: Enhancing User Experience and Performance

The theme for this phase is refinement – it's all about enhancing the visitor experience with improvements to areas such as language localization and the UI. I've listed some example areas and tasks in Table 5-2.

Table 5-2. *The Enhancing User Experience task list*

Area	Task(s)
Performance Optimization	Implement ISR (Incremental Static Regeneration) to serve pages quickly and optimize caching for multilingual content
Voice Search Refinements	Improve recognition of different accents and languages Test real-world use cases (e.g., noisy environments, mobile vs. desktop) Implement error handling for misrecognized speech
Localization Improvements	Format numbers, dates, and currencies dynamically Handle pluralization and grammatical nuances for each language
Navigation and UX Enhancements	Improve accessibility (ARIA labels, screen reader support) Ensure RTL support if needed

Phase 3: Advanced Features and Compliance

The third and final theme is advanced – this one covers those tasks that are more advanced or require checking for compliance. Examples include making sure SEO tags are long-tail and compliant, as well as checking for accessibility. I've listed some example areas and tasks in Table 5-3.

Table 5-3. *The Advanced Features task list*

Area	Task(s)
Advanced SEO and Ranking Improvements	Expand voice search optimization with long-tail keywords Use structured data (FAQ Schema, HowTo Schema) to boost rankings
Legal and Compliance Checks	Ensure GDPR compliance for voice search (if storing/transmitting audio) Verify accessibility compliance for screen readers
Testing and Monitoring	Set up Cypress tests for Speech API accuracy and multilingual search Track user behavior (are they using voice search frequently?) Collect feedback and iterate based on real-world usage

Although we've covered a host of different sample tasks – of which some may or may not apply to your setup – there is one point I need to reiterate: not all of this is a one-off.

I know that some people may not see the need to treat this work as ongoing and that they (for whatever reason it might be) might only be prepared to complete it once and then move on to other things. It isn't a recommended approach, though: granted, there are some things you only need to do once, such as setting up the voice feature in your codebase, as we did in our example.

Where this "one-time" approach will fail is that once voice search is in place, VSO can affect strategy in the future, and if we don't regularly review it, we might end up affecting performance, revenue, and the user experience:

- If we add new features to our site, we must review performance to ensure they haven't affected existing features. The Speech API is CPU intensive, so it pays to keep on top of performance!

- Changes in the local dialect and conversational speech can affect whether the API will understand a request – for example, some regions of France tend to use abbreviations, such as "sympa" for "sympathique" (pleasing or sympathetic in English). You might also see some regions (such as Alsace) use Germanic terms such as nonante (for ninety; quatre-vingt-dix in standard French), a variation shaped by Alsace's alternating periods under French and German rule, which left lasting traces on local speech.

- We also need to review SEO terms we use regularly – this is something we should do anyway for traditional SEO. Still, the addition of voice makes it more meaningful, especially when we don't want to be seen as discriminatory to anyone with special needs.

Excellent – now we have some idea of what to cover and in what order, plus we've revisited the need to review our changes regularly – let's get back to coding!

For the rest of this chapter, we will create a proof-of-concept showing how to incorporate international voice control into a voice search optimization-enabled site. This time around, we're going to mix things up a little and use TypeScript – this is just to provide a little variety and that we're not limited to standard React or vanilla JavaScript for our demos.

Building Our Demo

For our demo, we will fake a search box that returns the title of a blog post based on the search hint we enter into the search box. This feature would be perfect for a site that maintains a social media element like company news.

Now – before you ask, implementing a full-on search is probably a little out of scope for this book! However, we can cheat a little: I've taken inspiration from a demo created by Emmanuel Efavero (at `https://github.com/emanuelefavero/nextjs-search-query`), which uses JSON to act as a dummy source.

It makes it a little easier to assemble our demo – hopefully, it will show that it doesn't matter where the data comes from; we can still search for and display it using the power of voice, no matter what language we use. For this demo, I'm making a few assumptions:

- The demo uses functionality from Emmanuel's original demo, but I've rewritten my version from the ground up to use Next.js version 15/React 19 (it was written for Next 13.x).

- I will use English (for obvious reasons!), but I will also include French and Dutch as my extra languages.

- The demo will use the new App Router functionality from Next 15 rather than the standard Pages functionality.

Okay, with this in mind, let's dive in and look at setting up the site.

Setting Up the Base Site

Before we get stuck into developing our POC, there are a few things we need to bear in mind:

- The demo is a proof of concept (POC) only, so it won't be perfect: it's aimed at showing what internationalization could look like and highlighting the challenges we face!

- As this is a POC, we will not optimize the code, so this is something that we'll need to consider if we implement anything into production.

- We will switch things up a bit and use TypeScript in this demo, which will add a little variety to the demo.

- The site won't look like the one we worked on in previous chapters – this is more to keep things simple so you can see what we need to add or change to get everything working.

- Not everything will work immediately after each part of the demo – you will need to work through all of them for it to operate as expected.

With this in mind, let's begin with the first part of the POC, which is building the skeleton for our site.

There is a lot to cover in this demo, so we'll work through it block by block – feel free to pause at any time between each part!

BUILDING A POC – PART 1: THE BASIC SITE

To create the basis for our POC, follow these steps:

1. First, crack open a new terminal session, then change to the root of C: drive.

2. We will use create-next-app to create the basic skeleton of our site. To do this, enter the following at the prompt and press Enter:

```
npx create-next-app@latest next-search-lang
```

If it's not installed on your system, you may see a prompt to install
create-next-app, so hit Y.

3. Wait a few moments – you should see questions appear
    with Yes or No prompts. When prompted, select (Y)es for the
    following; all others leave as default or (N)o:

```
$ npx create-next-app@latest next-search-lang
√ Would you like to use TypeScript? ... No / Yes
√ Would you like to use ESLint? ... No / Yes
√ Would you like to use Tailwind CSS? ... No / Yes
√ Would you like your code inside a `src/` directory?
  ... No / Yes
√ Would you like to use App Router? (recommended) ...
  No / Yes
√ Would you like to use Turbopack for `next dev`? ...
  No / Yes
√ Would you like to customize the import alias
  (`@/*` by default)? ... No / Yes
```

You may find you can press Enter to accept the defaults.

4. Once complete, change into the new folder. We need to run the
    install process, so at the prompt, enter npm i and hit Enter.

5. We have more installation to do, which is next-intl. This
    package is one of the options available for internationalization
    in Next.js (and will play a key role in our demo). Revert to the
    prompt, then enter npm i next-intl at the prompt and
    press Enter.

6. We should see something similar to this appear in
    package.json to confirm successful installation:

    ```
    "next-intl": "^3.26.3",
    ```

7. We're almost done – with the basics now in place, let's fire up
    the site to make sure it's running. Enter npm run dev to fire
    up the development server at the terminal session prompt, then
    press Enter.

8. Wait for it to run up the server – you should see confirmation
    it's ready to run momentarily, similar to this:

    ```
    ▲ Next.js 15.1.6
    - Local:        http://localhost:3000
    - Network:      http://192.168.1.160:3000
    ```

9. Go ahead and browse to http://localhost:3000 – if all is
    well, we should see the site appear, as shown in Figure 5-1.

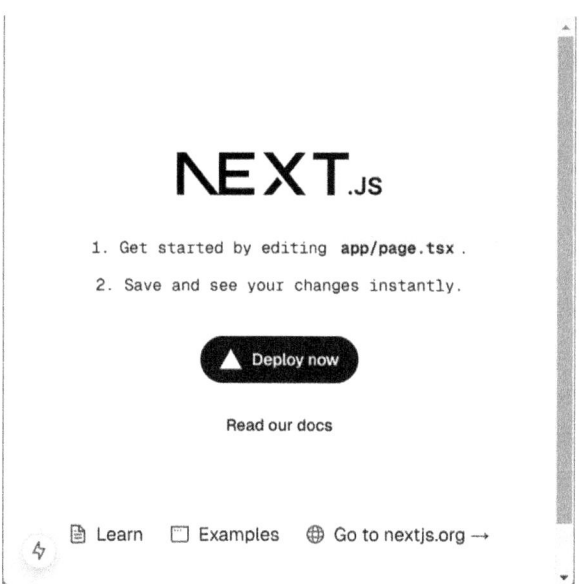

Figure 5-1. *Confirmation that the base skeleton of the POC is running*

171

Excellent – but this is just the start! We now have the base skeleton of our site in place, and we are ready to add the various pages throughout this chapter. Before we start that process, let's take a moment to review what we created in that last demo in more detail.

Understanding the Changes Made

If you've spent time with React, Svelte, Vue (or even NextJS!), you will be familiar with the process we used in the last exercise – scaffolding.

For those unfamiliar with it, scaffolding is not covering your home with metal poles before building work but installing a single app that sets up a barebones project, ready for us to use. Sure, it will install some predetermined packages, but we can control this by what we choose to install. The good thing is that we know it's a tried and tested system that provides a consistent setup for us.

By default, create-next-app (CNA) installs the basic packages we need for Next to run: React and React-DOM. During the installation, we chose to use the App Router template, plus several packages; an extract of what is installed is shown below:

```
Installing dependencies:
- react
- react-dom
- next

Installing devDependencies:
- typescript
- @types/node
- @types/react
- @types/react-dom
- eslint
- eslint-config-next
- @eslint/eslintrc
```

At the same time, we also installed the `next-intl` package (available from `https://next-intl.dev/`). This step prepares us for setting up the international support we will add to our demo in this chapter. To finish off this demo, we ran up the development server before navigating to the site to ensure it displays as expected in the browser.

Okay, let's move on! We now have a basic skeleton of a site, which uses the out-of-the-box Next.js 15 configuration plus the extra next-intl package we installed for language support. The next task will be to configure it, but before we do so, we should cover a few points concerning the packages we use and some of the points to consider around locale support.

Implementing Language Support

This is where things get interesting!

Implementing *basic* language support in itself is very easy, but there are points we have to consider, particularly around the use of packages and how far we want to take the process. What do I mean by this? Let me explain.

Notice how I mentioned the word basic in italics at the start of that last paragraph – this was with good reason. Installing a package for internationalization is straightforward; we use an npm package, which follows the standard process for all npm packages. Where things get tricky is that we have a few questions to answer around configuration specifics:

- Are we using Next.js 13+ or standard React?

- How will we source translations?

- What is our preference for recognizing locales? Should this be automatic or manual?

- What changes will we need to accommodate any static or dynamic content?

- How will our choices impact SEO, such as using locale folders or subdomains?

- Which labels should we translate, such as buttons, fieldsets, and the like?

- Have we determined which languages to support and whether any country markets prefer specific languages or their everyday language?

Wow – this one could send your head spinning! To help slow it down, let me contextualize some of these questions so you can understand what decisions you need to make when adding the language changes to your projects. I've listed both in no particular order in Table 5-4.

Table 5-4. *Questions and context around adding language support*

Questions	Context
Are we using Next.js 13+ or standard React?	For Next 15, next-intl is required for support, while older versions or plain React can use next-i18next or react-intl
How will we source translations?	For translated content, native speakers are ideal, but AI or Google may be options with privacy in mind. Integration depends on the source, with CMS or databases for updates and static blocks for stable content
What is our preference around recognizing locales – should this be automatic or manual?	This is around whether we want to provide an option to switch locales manually (say EN to NL and vice versa) or use the power of the repo to do this automatically, based on detecting a locale in the URL

(continued)

Table 5-4. (*continued*)

Questions	Context
What changes will we need to accommodate any static or dynamic content?	This could be a little tricky – some of the content will be easy to update, but other areas, such as metadata tags, will be more challenging! These changes may also cause other issues, such as hydration – I'll touch on this later in the chapter
How will our choices impact SEO, such as using locale folders or subdomains?	Some of this will be determined by what may already be in place – Next.js supports the use of /en, /de, and the like, but what if we want to use something like en.yoursite.com?
Which text should we translate, such as for buttons or labels?	This depends on translation storage – CMS for easy updates or manual changes. Tasks should be manageable to reduce impact. Updating all at once is faster but riskier; smaller batches are safer but slower
Have we decided on supported languages and are there any country-specific preferences?	In the main, this should be straightforward, as business needs will drive it; the only real question is whether any market prefers a language different from one you would expect, such as English for Denmark instead of Danish

There's plenty there to think about and drive conversations – in the meantime, let's look at implementing the next batch of changes to our demo so we can get ever closer to a working example of adding language support for VSO.

PART 2: ADDING LOCALIZED PAGE AND SEARCH

To build out our POC, follow these steps:

1. First, we need to replace the existing home page with our search example. For this, create a new folder called [locale] at the root of \app.

2. Next, create a new file called layout.tsx inside the [locale] folder – go ahead and add this code. We have a fair bit to cover, so we'll do it in blocks, starting with two imports:

```
import { ReactNode } from "react";
import LanguageSwitcher from "@/app/components/
LanguageSwitcher";
```

3. Next, leave a line blank, then add this function – this takes care of adding a title and description as an introduction to our app POC:

```
export function generateMetadata({ params }: { params:
{ locale?: string } }) {
  if (!params || !params.locale) {
    return {
      title: "Multilingual Search",
      description: "A demo site for multilingual search
      using Next.js 15.",
    };
  }
```

```
return {
  title: `Multilingual Search - ${params.locale.
  toUpperCase()}`,
  description: "A demo site for multilingual search
  using Next.js 15.",
  };
}
```

4. For the last part of `layout.tsx`, we need to add the main return block – add this code immediately below the last line from step 3:

```
export default function LocaleLayout({
  children,
  params,
}: {
  children: ReactNode;
  params: { locale: string };
}) {
  return (
    <html lang={params.locale} suppressHydrationWarning>
      <body>
        <LanguageSwitcher />
        {children}
      </body>
    </html>
  );
}
```

5.   Save and close the file. Next, create a new file called `Page.tsx` in the `\app\[locale]` folder; this will be the main page we display in our POC. There is a lot to cover, so as before, we'll do it in sections starting with an import and defining a `translations` object – the first part of which contains the translations for English:

```
import Search from "@/app/components/Search";

const translations = {
  en: {
    metaTitle: "Search Posts",
    metaDescription: "Find posts in your selected
    language.",
    selectedLanguage: "Selected language: EN",
    searchHint: 'Try searching for "first", "second",
    or "third" post.',
  },
```

6.   The second part contains the text to display for Dutch language:

```
  nl: {
    metaTitle: "Zoek Berichten",
    metaDescription: "Vind berichten in uw
    geselecteerde taal.",
    selectedLanguage: "Geselecteerde taal: NL",
    searchHint: 'Probeer te zoeken naar "eerste",
    "tweede" of "derde" bericht.',
  },
```

7.   The third and final part contains the text for French language:

```
  fr: {
    metaTitle: "Rechercher des Articles",
    metaDescription: "Trouvez des articles dans votre
    langue sélectionnée.",
```

```
   selectedLanguage: "Langue sélectionnée : FR",
   searchHint:
     'Essayez de rechercher "premier", "deuxième" ou
     "troisième" article.',
 },
};
```

8. Next, leave a line blank, then add this function, which will
    render the relevant title, description, and search hint depending
    on which language is selected:

```
export default async function Home({ params }: {
params: { locale: string } }) {
  const { locale } = await Promise.resolve(params);
  const messages = translations[locale] ||
  translations["en"]; // Fallback to English

  return (
    <main>
      <h1>{messages.metaTitle}</h1>
      <p>{messages.selectedLanguage}</p>
      <p className="search-hint">{messages.
      searchHint}</p>
      <Search />
    </main>
  );
}
```

9. Save and close the file. We have one more file to add, which is
    route.ts. For this, create two folders. The first is api at the
    root level, and then inside that folder, create one called search.

10. With the folders in place, crack open a new file and add this
     code – we'll add it in blocks, starting with importing two
     functions, creating two TypeScript interfaces, and adding a
     posts constant:

```
import { NextResponse } from "next/server";
import postsData from "@/app/data/posts.json";

interface Post {
  id: string;
  title: string;
}

interface PostsData {
  en: Post[];
  nl: Post[];
  fr: Post[];
}

// Ensure postsData is correctly typed
const posts: PostsData = postsData as PostsData;
```

11. We then come to the main function in this component, which
     gets the locale from the posted URL and filters out posts that do
     not match the query:

```
export async function GET(req: Request) {
  const { searchParams } = new URL(req.url);
  const query = searchParams.get("q")?.
  toLowerCase() || "";
  const lang = (searchParams.get("lang") as keyof
  PostsData) || "en";
```

```
if (!query) {
  return NextResponse.json(
    { error: "Missing query parameter `q`" },
    { status: 400 }
  );
}

// Ensure lang is valid
if (!posts[lang]) {
  return NextResponse.json(
    { error: "Invalid language parameter" },
    { status: 400 }
  );
}

// Apply correct typing to `post`
const filteredPosts = posts[lang].filter((post:
Post) =>
  post.title.toLowerCase().includes(query)
);
return NextResponse.json(filteredPosts);
}
```

12. Save and close all open files – we'll reconvene with the next part of the demo shortly.

Excellent – well done if you've made it so far, given how much we covered in that last demo! I know we've not yet run up the work done so far in a browser, but that's something I found when building this demo: a lot of the core code is challenging to split easily so that we can see changes coming in while still maintaining functionality. I'll come back to that later, but for now, let's take a moment to review the changes we've made so far before adding two components needed for our demo in the next exercise.

Breaking Apart the Changes

So, what did we achieve in part two of our demo?

This demo was primarily about adding locale support – the key is to remember that although we have a root layout template, we use a localized template for each of the different locales in our demo.

First, we created a [locale] folder for our demo, into which we added first a layout.tsx component. It uses the generateMetadata method to set up and render the SEO metadata on our page before rendering it (and our targeted locale ID) the <head> markup on our page.

The tags are semi-hardcoded for now, as they presented something of an issue – I'll come back to this a little later in the chapter.

Next, we then created the localized page.tsx file – this renders the content of our demo in the browser. We started by setting up a translations object containing each locale's various labels before adding the Home() function that displays content on the page. This function references the relevant translations based on first resolving a Promise that contains the locale parameter, then filtering out the translations not required for our locale.

It's interesting to note that if translations[locale] is null, it will default to translations[en], which is English.

For the last part of this demo, we created route.ts – this takes care of fetching the data from the posts.json data file before working out which locale we are targeting in the GET function and filtering out anything that doesn't match the locale. So, in this case, if we had chosen to go to http://localhost:3000/nl, this would pick up nl as the locale and render filteredposts with the content from the nl object in our JSON file.

Adding the Search Facility

So far, we've made great progress with assembling our demo, but we still have work to do!

This next part covers two critical components for our demo. We need a language switcher to change languages at will, and the main search component will return data filtered based on the term we enter into the search field. Fortunately, this shouldn't be too complicated to set up, so let's begin with the next exercise, which should bring us closer to our working demo.

PART 3: ADDING THE MAIN COMPONENTS

To add the key functionality to our site, follow these steps:

1. First, we need somewhere to store these components – go ahead and create a new folder called `components` in the `\app` folder of our repo.

2. Next, crack open a new file, then add this code, allowing us to switch between different languages. We'll be adding a nice chunk of code, which we will do block by block, starting with importing four functions from React and Next:

```
"use client";

import { useEffect, useState } from "react";
import { usePathname, useRouter } from "next/
navigation";
```

3. Next up is the main switcher function:

```
export default function LanguageSwitcher() {
  const router = useRouter();
  const pathname = usePathname();
```

```
const [hydrated, setHydrated] = useState(false);
useEffect(() => {
  setHydrated(true); // Ensure component only renders
  after hydration
}, []);

if (!hydrated) return null; // Avoid mismatches by
not rendering during SSR

function switchLanguage(newLang: string) {
  const segments = pathname.split("/").
  filter(Boolean);
  segments[0] = newLang;
  router.push(`/${segments.join("/")}`);
}
```

4. The last part of this component takes care of rendering the UI for our language switcher:

```
return (
  <div className="switcher">
    <button onClick={() => switchLanguage("en")}>GB
    EN</button>
    <button onClick={() => switchLanguage("nl")}>NL
    NL</button>
    <button onClick={() => switchLanguage("fr")}>FR
    FR</button>
  </div>
);
}
```

5. Save the file as LanguageSwitcher.tsx, then close it.

6. We now need to add the main search component – for this, crack open a new file, and save it as `Search.tsx` in the \ `components` folder. Add this code block by block, starting with two imports and defining a type interface:

```
"use client";

import { useState, useEffect } from "react";
import { usePathname } from "next/navigation";

type Post = {
  id: string;
  title: string;
};
```

7. Next, leave a line blank, then add the first part of the `Search()` function, which defines a set of constants for use in the component:

```
export default function Search() {
  const pathname = usePathname();
  const [query, setQuery] = useState("");
  const [results, setResults] = useState<Post[]>([]);
  const [lang, setLang] = useState<string |
  null>(null);
  const [hydrated, setHydrated] = useState(false);
```

8. Next comes a `useEffect()` – this picks up the language locale and adds it to state:

```
useEffect(() => {
  setHydrated(true); // Mark as hydrated
  const segments = pathname.split("/").filter(Boolean);
```

```
    if (segments.length > 0) {
      setLang(segments[0]);
    }
  }, [pathname]);
```

9. This next function takes care of retrieving the data from the
    posts JSON file and filters it according to the locale set:

```
async function handleSearch(e: React.
FormEvent<HTMLFormElement>) {
  e.preventDefault();
  if (!query || !lang) return;

  const response = await fetch(`/api/search?q=
${query}&lang=${lang}`);
  const data = await response.json();
  setResults(data);
}
```

10. The last part of this component takes care of rendering the UI
    for our Search facility:

```
if (!hydrated || !lang) return null;

return (

    <form onSubmit={handleSearch}>
      <input
        type="text"
        value={query}
        onChange={(e) => setQuery(e.target.value)}
        placeholder="Search posts"
      />
      <button type="submit">Search</button>
    </form>
```

```
<ul>
  {results.map((post) => (
    <li key={post.id}>{post.title}</li>
  ))}
</ul>
);
}
```

11. Save and close the file – we'll complete the rest of the demo shortly.

Perfect – adding these two components brings us one step closer to completing our demo. We've covered some practical concepts in this exercise, so before we move on to the fourth and final part of this demo, let's take a moment to explore the changes we made in more detail.

Exploring the Changes

One of the things I've noticed about setting up this demo is how tricky it has been to find ways of slicing up the work into sensible parcels or Agile stories. It's why we've not been able to run up the demo after each exercise – it's not ideal, but it highlights the important point that we will need to consider what changes we implement and when! That said, I completed two key parts in this demo – adding two components, LanguageSwitcher and Search. Let's take a look at the first in more detail.

LanguageSwitcher does precisely as it says on the tin: to set the target locale as our chosen language. When we click the chosen language button, we pass in the locale to the switchLanguage function before assembling the target URL and pushing it into the router. It will trigger a change of URL, with the browser swapping over content to the new locale. It's important to note that we only render this component when everything has been hydrated. Otherwise, we will end up with hydration errors in the browser!

In the second component, we create the core part of our demo – Search. We set up several constants for state, such as `hydrated`/`setHydrated` and `query`/`setQuery`. We then extract the current locale and store this in state, before building the main `handleSearch` event handler.

Here, we string together the fetch statement using the `q` and `lang` values before fetching the contents and assigning the JSON block to `data`. Throughout this function, we also set `hydrated` to `true` or `false`, depending on when we want to re-render the display. We finish this part of the demo by building the markup that renders the language buttons on the screen and the event handler to submit changes when someone clicks a language button in the browser.

Completing the Rest of the Build

The last part of this marathon exercise is a nice short one compared to some of the previous tasks! In this one, we need to add two more files: a layout template and a simple middleware function to redirect to the correct locale in the browser.

At the same time, we will pull some files from the code download; these will still play an important role but are less critical to the whole operation! Let's dive in and add the last part so we can begin to see the demo in action and add new functionality to it later in the chapter.

PART 4: ADDING THE REMAINING FILES

To complete the build of our demo, follow these steps:

1. For the first task, we need to add a layout template to our demo – crack open the existing `layout.tsx` file at the root of `\app`, then replace the contents of it with this code:

```
import type { Metadata } from "next";
import "./globals.css";

export const metadata: Metadata = {
  title: "Create Next App",
  description: "Generated by create next app",
};

export default function RootLayout({
  children,
}: {
  children: React.ReactNode;
}) {
  return (
    <html lang="en">
      <body>{children}</body>
    </html>
  );
}
```

2. Save the file, then close it.

3. Open a new file, and add this block of code – this will redirect
    the URL in the browser if no locale tag is specified in the URL:

```
import { NextResponse } from "next/server";
import type { NextRequest } from "next/server";

export function middleware(request: NextRequest) {
  const { pathname } = request.nextUrl;
```

```
if (pathname === "/") {
  return NextResponse.redirect(new URL("/en",
  request.url));
}

return NextResponse.next();
}
```

4. Save the file as `middleware.ts` at the root of the repo.

5. We have three more files to add, but we can get these from this book's code download – `posts.json`, `translations.js`, and an updated styling file, `globals.css`. The first two should go into a folder called `data` at the root of the repo; the `globals.css` file can stay at the root level.

You may need to create the data folder if it is not present. I've also left the existing styles in `global.css` as they are for now; this is a POC, so they are not essential to the demo, and you can remove them if you wish.

You will be pleased to hear that we have reached the end of this marathon build! We've covered a lot of code in the last few mini demos; hopefully, this will give you a flavor of what we need to add language support (and ultimately link it to voice, which we will do later in this chapter).

Before we move on to the next part of this project, let's take a moment to test our demo works before understanding some of the finer points and challenges we will face when scaling this into a bigger product.

Understanding What Happened

The last part of our demo was a real ragbag of changes – none of them fall into any particular category, but all are still required!

The first of the changes was to update the root layout file with new code – we removed what was provided out of the box and replaced it with new code that includes importing Next, a stylesheet, and creating a `metadata` block for SEO tags.

We then moved on to adding a `middleware.ts` function – the purpose of this is to act as a fallback redirect if no locale is displayed in the URL. If the URL does not include one of the known locales, it redirects to `/en` as our default locale. We finished the demo by pulling in some extra files from the code download (a stylesheet, a translations block, and a JSON data file) – all play a valuable role but are less critical than the files we've covered throughout our multipart demo.

Testing the Demo

Finally, it's time to test our demo!

I know it's been a long time coming, but adding language support is a task that isn't easy to split without significant changes to existing content or affecting existing functionality in a site.

It's why this kind of change is always better done as part of a greenfield project, but we live in reality – this isn't always possible. It means that we have to be careful about how we implement each part; it may require us to put changes into production that we can't see or activate until we add more changes at a later date.

Leaving that all aside for a moment, I bet you're dying to see what we've done and whether it all works, so without further ado, let's get in and crank up our demo.

TESTING THE PROOF OF CONCEPT

To test the demo, follow these steps:

1. Switch to a Node.js terminal session, then make sure the working folder is set to our project area.

2. At the prompt, enter `npm run dev` and press Enter. Wait a few moments, then when prompted, browse to `http://localhost:3000`.

3. Notice that it redirects automatically to your locale or `http://localhost:3000/en` as the default.

This happens for me as English is my locale, but it will happen for you as your default locale. If you live in a French or Dutch locale, you may find it redirecting to those instead.

---

4. If all is well, we should see something akin to this screenshot (Figure 5-2).

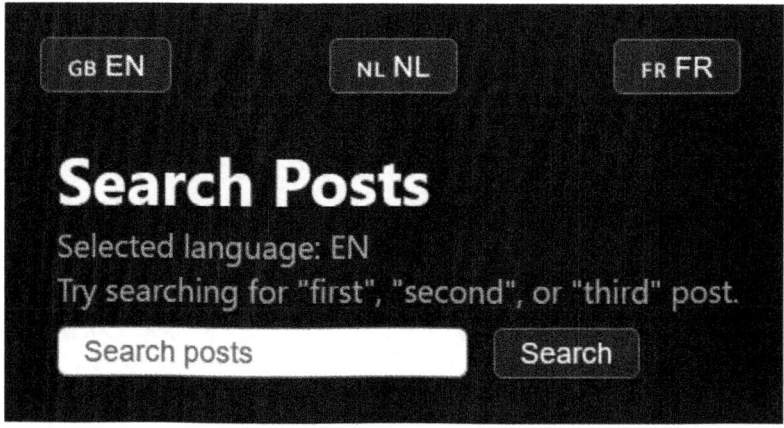

Figure 5-2. *The English locale version of the demo*

5. Try clicking either nl NL or fr FR — we should see the page change without refreshing to display whichever language you chose. Here's what the Dutch one looks like as an example (Figure 5-3).

Figure 5-3. *The Dutch version of our demo*

6. For completeness, here's how the French demo looks
   (Figure 5-4).

Figure 5-4. *The French version of our demo*

At last! We have a working demo to which we can now add voice support. I know that will be significantly easier to achieve. However, doing the vocal tests could be a real test of whether I can speak Dutch and – more importantly – whether the demo and speech facility will understand someone whose mother tongue isn't Dutch (or French, for that matter!).

Before we add the speech capability, I want to spend a few moments reviewing the code we've created in our demo. While creating the demo as part of my original research, I've noticed a few challenges that may affect how you implement these changes into a proper project. It would be worth going through these in more detail so you get a feel for them, and we can go through any possible options at the same time.

Exploring the Challenges

Life is like a box of chocolates – you never know what ya gonna get....

The movie buffs among you may recognize that line from the famous movie Forrest Gump – I know I can't show the accent in print (yet – but one can hope), but those words portrayed by Tom Hanks could be a bit of a metaphor for what we have seen so far with implementing VSO.

Don't get me wrong – I'm only referring to what we see in our POC, not what eventually goes into production! The point here, though, is that the internationalization work we've done has thrown up some challenges we need to be aware of, so let's go some of what I've found.

The most critical issue I've seen is one of hydration errors appearing in the console, some of which started like this:

```
<OuterLayoutRouter parallelRouterKey="children"
segmentPath={[...]} template={<RenderFromTemplateContext>} ...>
  <RenderFromTemplateContext>
    <ScrollAndFocusHandler segmentPath={[...]}>
...
```

These were coming from differences between the client and server rendering of our site and could be caused by several reasons, such as Next. js re-rendering content once it's processed the stylesheet or switching from the root layout to the locale layout files.

I experimented with changes to see if I could fix it but to no avail. I think this has highlighted that working with one layout template rather than multiple ones will be better. For now, I added the suppressHydrationWarning tag to stop it from showing as a temporary measure, but this isn't without its challenges:

- This tag should only be used as a last resort, as it can hide legitimate hydration errors appearing from other features on the page. We can get away with it for now as we have a small, controlled mismatch showing that doesn't affect our functionality.

- The other challenge is that we do have dynamic content in play on the client, but it is consistent on the server – it means that we'd have to watch out for inconsistencies between both *if* we were to use the suppressHydrationWarning tag in production.

It wasn't the only challenge I found – a few others popped up for me, which you could see appear in your projects. Let's have a look at them:

- Meta tags were not always correct, which will impact SEO. A lot of this will come from issues I saw with adding dynamic data to the generateMetadata() function, but this is not dynamic: to get around this, could we combine layouts into one? It means that we have to consider whether we use multiple layouts or just one – I don't want it to stifle choice, but at the same time, we need to be mindful of not adding errors unnecessarily!

- You will no doubt have seen that the code I've used is not optimized for DRYness; it's OK for a proof of concept, but we would need to go through and optimize it properly before releasing it into production. At the same time, we need to work out what we can add and when to slice up the work into manageable stories without impacting the site.

- We incorporated the translations into the code base to prove they work: How will we manage updating content? Will it be via a CMS so others can assist, or must it be a code release change?

- In connection with the issue around SEO, we assumed /en, /fr, and /nl was the best format, but does this match how your site is set up (or will be set up?)

- The language switcher is hardcoded for now, but we will need to make this dynamic; can we pull these values in from the backend (based on what languages it detects), or do we still need to provide a hard-coded block of locales?

Hopefully, this will give us something to consider – I don't want to end up with a long list of issues as that sounds negative. But equally, if we encounter any challenges, we should work out if they need fixing and prioritize them accordingly!

Okay, at this point, let's change focus: we have the demo in place and have covered some of the challenges you might encounter. It's time now to add the most crucial part: voice support! Fortunately, we've already done a part of this with the code we added back in Chapter 4; we can start to use the same principles in this demo.

Updating the Voice Input

IT's time to get vocal…!

Okay, that's a terrible joke, but in all seriousness, we've now reached the point where we can add voice support to our demo.

Although services are available to help with this, such as Google Cloud Speech-to-Text or Microsoft Azure's Cognitive Services, staying with the Speech API we used back in Chapter 4 makes sense.

The reason for this is that while it may not be as finely tuned as the paid-for services, it is at least free – one of the downsides of using a third-party service is that it could get expensive, depending on how much demand you have on your site! Using the built-in browser option as our starting point, we can establish whether it works and what benefits we get. We can use this to build a case for upgrading to a paid-for service later if we outgrow what is available in the browser.

Whatever happens, we need to be mindful of accuracy, particularly when it comes to accents and regional differences – it will pay to have a native speaker help with testing! We may find that if the browser option doesn't include a particular dialect or has poor support for a region, this will dictate what we do and how we grow what we offer to our customers.

As an aside, it may be worth building an internal service to help with translation. I know using automated services can be risky, given that they won't include the intonation or specifics of a dialect, but it will be a good starting point!

Okay, let's move on and start coding. For this demo, we'll add a button to enable the microphone when needed and set it to search as soon as it records and displays a term. It will also automatically shut off after ten minutes, so we're not trapping conversations indefinitely! Let's dive in and take a look at the changes we need to make to get voice support working for our demo.

As an aside – I'm using the microphone icon from `https://www.iconfinder.com/icons/326557/mic_icon` for this demo; please feel free to swap it out if you like. I recommend a size of 24px square – you will need to edit the SVG markup in the VoiceSearch component if you decide to change it.

ADJUSTING THE VOICE SUPPORT

To add voice support, follow these steps:

1. First, we need to install a package that will add type support for the SpeechRecognition API. For this, crack open a Node.js terminal, and change the working folder to our project folder.

2. At the prompt, enter `npm i --save-dev @types/dom-speech-recognition`, and hit Enter – wait for it to install.

3. Once installed, we need to restart the TypeScript server – I use VS Code, so for this, it's Shift+Ctrl+P to bring up the command palette, then enter `restart` and choose the `TypeScript: Restart TS Server` option.

If you're using a different editor, you should have a similar option – please check online to confirm details.

4. First, we need to add a speech component – for this, crack open your editor, then create a new file called `VoiceSearch.tsx`, in the root of the `\apps\components` folder.

5. In the file, add the following code – there is a fair bit to cover, so we'll do it in blocks, starting with an import and defining some TypeScript interfaces:

```
import { useState, useEffect } from 'react';

declare global {
  interface Window {
    SpeechRecognition: typeof SpeechRecognition;
    webkitSpeechRecognition: typeof SpeechRecognition;
  }
}
```

199

```
interface VoiceSearchProps {
  onSearch: (query: string) => void;
  onLanguageSwitch: (lang: string) => void;
}
```

6. Next, we'll open the main VoiceSearch function for the component – here, we set some constants to store data in state:

```
const VoiceSearch = ({ onSearch,
onLanguageSwitch }) => {
    const [isListening, setIsListening] =
    useState(false);
    const [recognition, setRecognition] =
    useState(null);
    const [silenceTimer, setSilenceTimer] =
    useState(null);
```

7. Next, leave a line blank, then add this useEffect() block – this defines the SpeechRecognition object, with changes applied when any changes in searching or chosen language are detected:

```
useEffect(() => {
  if (typeof window !== "undefined") {
    const SpeechRecognition =
      window.SpeechRecognition || window.
      webkitSpeechRecognition;

    if (SpeechRecognition) {
      const recognitionInstance = new
      SpeechRecognition();
      recognitionInstance.continuous = true;
```

```
recognitionInstance.interimResults = false;
recognitionInstance.lang = "en";

recognitionInstance.onresult = (event:
SpeechRecognitionEvent) => {
  const transcript =
    event.results[event.results.length - 1][0].
    transcript.trim();
  console.log("Transcript:", transcript);

  if (transcript.toLowerCase().
  startsWith("switch to")) {
    const newLang = transcript.split("switch to
    ")[1]?.trim();
    if (newLang) onLanguageSwitch(newLang);
  } else {
    onSearch(transcript);
  }
};

recognitionInstance.onstart = () =>
setListening(true);

recognitionInstance.onend = () => {
  setListening(false);
};

setRecognition(recognitionInstance);
    }
  }
}, [onSearch, onLanguageSwitch]);
```

8. This next block takes care of setting a 10-minute timeout on the SpeechRecognition feature if it detects it's not being used:

```
const startListening = () => {
  if (recognition) {
    recognition.start();
    setListening(true);

    if (timeoutId) clearTimeout(timeoutId);
    const id = window.setTimeout(() => {
      stopListening();
    }, 10 * 60 * 1000);
    setTimeoutId(id);
  }
};

const stopListening = () => {
  if (recognition) {
    recognition.stop();
    setListening(false);
    if (timeoutId) clearTimeout(timeoutId);
    setTimeoutId(null);
  }
};
```

9. Leave a line blank, then add the last part of the code – this shows a button with a microphone, ready for activation when needed:

```
return (
<button onClick={listening ? stopListening :
startListening}>
    <svg height="21px" version="1.1" viewBox="0 0 14
    21" width="14px">
```

```
    <g
      fill="none"
      fillRule="evenodd"
      id="Page-1"
      stroke="none"
      strokeWidth="1"
    >
      <g
        fill="#000000"
        id="Icons-AV"
        transform="translate(-3.000000, -43.000000)"
      >
        <g id="mic" transform="translate(3.000000,
        43.500000)">
          <path
            d="M7,12 C8.7,12 10,10.7 10,9 L10,3
            C10,1.3 8.7,0 7,0 C5.3,0 4,1.3 4,3 L4,9
            C4,10.7 5.3,12 7,12 L7,12 Z M12.3,9
            C12.3,12 9.8,14.1 7,14.1 C4.2,14.1 1.7,12
            1.7,9 L0,9 C0,12.4 2.7,15.2 6,15.7 L6,19
            L8,19 L8,15.7 C11.3,15.2 14,12.4 14,9
            L12.3,9 L12.3,9 Z"
            id="Shape"
          />
        </g>
      </g>
    </g>
  </svg>
</button>
  );
};
```

10. We have one more change to make – with the addition of our new microphone button, the styling is a little off! It won't harm performance, but it would be nice to get it right. To fix it, update the entry for `form` and add a new entry for `.microphone`, as shown:

```
form {
  margin-top: 10px;
  display: flex;
}
```

```
.microphone { margin-right: 10px; }
```

11. Save and close all files. Next, fire up a Node.js terminal session, then change the working folder to the project area (if it is not already there).

12. Enter `npm run dev` at the prompt, and press Enter to start the Next.js development server.

13. When prompted, browse to `http://localhost:3000` – if all is well, we should see the new button appear, as shown in Figure 5-5.

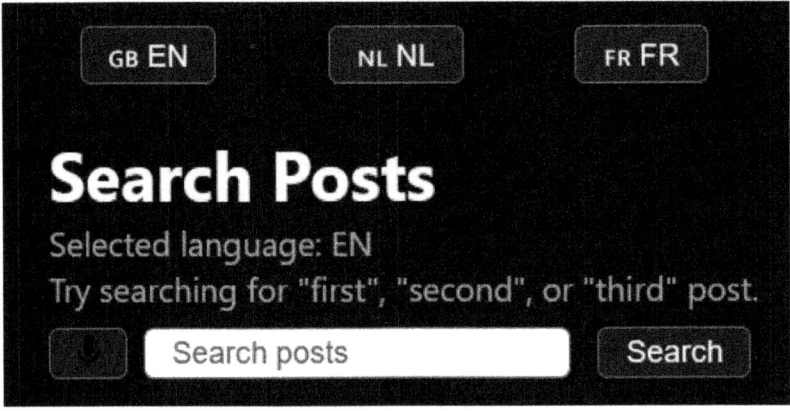

Figure 5-5. *Addition of the new speech button*

14.   Click the button to activate the speech facility – we should
       see a prompt to enable the microphone from the browser
       (Figure 5-6).

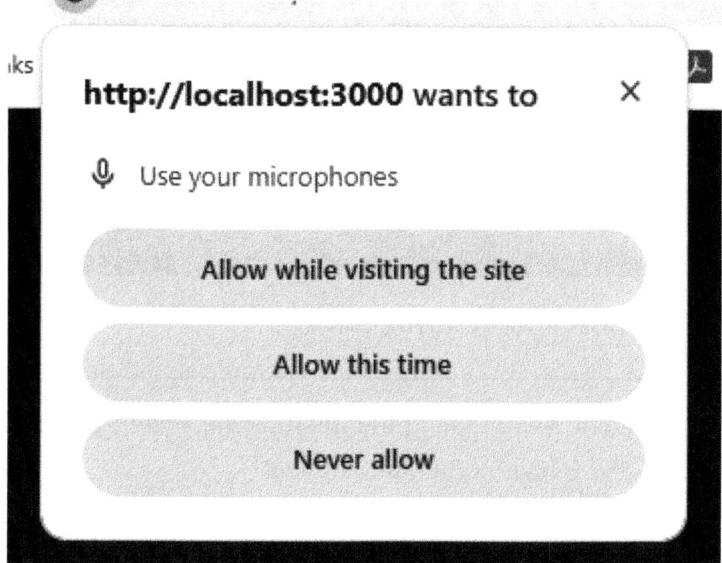

Figure 5-6. *Enabling the microphone in the browser*

15.   Select the top option, then try saying "first" in the microphone.

16.   We should see the word appear in the search box if all is well.
       It may take a few moments to happen, but once entered, it will
       automatically trigger the Search option to list the name of the
       post below it, as shown in Figure 5-7.

Figure 5-7. *The results of saying "first"*

Please be patient when testing the microphone – the transcript results can take a few moments to appear!

---

17. It's impossible to show this action in print, so to confirm that your microphone is working, look at the console log in the browser. You should see an entry for Transcript: appear, along with your spoken words, similar to the example shown in Figure 5-8.

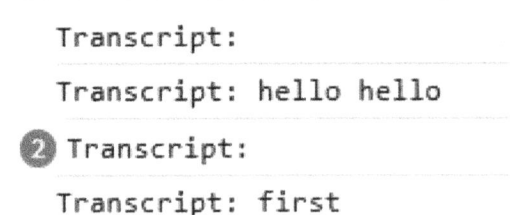

Figure 5-8. *Proof that our microphone is working*

Excellent – we now have a fully working demo that can search using your voice and has (albeit only partially) localized SEO! We've covered a lot of content in this demo, so before we move on to our next topic, let's take a breather for a moment and review the changes we made in more detail.

Exploring What Changed

Although the Speech API available in the browser is a jack of all trades, one thing it doesn't have is TypeScript support!

To fix this, we started by installing the `@types/dom-speech-recognition` package; the great thing is that we don't need to configure it, as it will silently work for us in the background. With this in place, we had to restart the TypeScript server in our editor so it could pick up the new bindings before we could add code.

Next, we added a new component called `VoiceSearch`, which provides the main voice recognition. The code we used is very similar to what we used back in Chapter 4 but with the addition of TypeScript types. We started by declaring two interfaces before creating the core component. This code includes initializing the `SpeechRecognition()` object as `recognitionInstance`, then specifying certain values such as `continuous` (checking for input all of the time), `interimResults` (here, only displaying the final result), and setting the supported language to English. At the same time, we created three event handlers – one to set `setListening` to true when starting the Speech API, one to shut it off when we're finished, and one to handle the output created by the API.

We then finished the demo by adding the markup for the Search option – most of this centers around a single button, but we include an SVG for the microphone icon. It is an important safety feature; we can't have the microphone running automatically due to privacy issues. To get around it, we can use the button to trigger the microphone when needed and then shut it off automatically at the end of a search. To prove it all works, we ran up the demo in a browser, clicked the button, and saw it activate before testing to see if it displayed text and triggered the search for us.

Great, our demo is working for us, and we can see what happens when we articulate a term in the demo. This, however, exposes some challenges for us that we should explore further:

- The API is not supported in IE, Firefox, or Opera – the first one shouldn't matter as IE is largely considered dead technology; the other two still get a little use, but it's below 1%. It's unlikely to impact revenue, but as always, you will need to check your analytics!

- You will notice that I touched on having a button to activate our microphone manually. This requirement is a security feature that prevents recording or transcribing conversations unless activated. Clicking this button will work for non-disabled people, but what about those with limited mobility?

- I've mentioned that the API is supported in some browsers, but not all: as part of this, we still need to use a Webkit vendor prefix for Chrome and Edge. Do we still need to use it, or can we get away without it? It might take some time before we can drop the vendor prefix though!

- I noticed that speed occasionally seems to be an issue, where the transcribed input doesn't always appear in the input field very quickly. I've not yet seen what is causing it or why – it is something we should investigate. Otherwise, customers will think it's not working! It may be a case of seeing if we can implement a "loading" indicator while it's still processing its input so visitors at least know if it's working.

- Although my demo is functional, some of the UX isn't ideal. For example, we could improve the styling of the microphone button to show whether it's active or inactive. I will return to this later in this chapter when we discuss working with stakeholders and UX design.

- There is an important point we need to address – reusability. The code we've implemented for the Speech API works but isn't very efficient! If you happen to work in a scenario where you might implement VSO in multiple projects, developing a mini library or abstract layer could be helpful. Adding one will make code more consistent, readable, and potentially easier to update as functionality develops in the browser. At the same time, we can include a layer that exposes options such as showing interim results and target language, making it easier to configure. If we wanted to, we could even create an NPM package for it, although making it public might be less desirable if it contains proprietary information for a company!

I know this is just a small set of some of the challenges you may face – the key here is to keep dialogue going between all parties so that we all understand what is needed and can implement it correctly in our environment.

Okay, let's crack on: when we set up our demo, we included a couple of ways to access each locale. The first is by going directly to a link (i.e., `http://localhost:3000/en` to the English site); the second is by clicking a button to redirect to a new locale. However, there is an alternative that could potentially be better for customers: geolocation. You may see it if you hit a site like Amazon.com from a different country, and it encourages you to go to your own country's site.

This feature is worth looking at for your site – to see how you might achieve it, look at the PDF I've created, which is in the code download for this book. The styling might not be stunning, but it should give you an idea of how we could add something functional to your projects!

Optimizing Performance

We've almost reached the end of our journey, but we still need to address two areas – one of which we've already visited, and the other is not one we've touched on yet. Let's go back to the one we visited first: optimization.

Some of you may say this is something we did back in Chapter 3, and you'd be right ... but only to an extent. The reason for this is that with the new language options in place, there is still scope for us to optimize our site, particularly around rendering translations.

There is a challenge, though: we added our translations directly into the front end, which may not be appropriate for your setup. This said, there are a couple of strategies worth exploring in Next.js, which could help:

- If our translations are static (which they are), we can pre-render the pages on the server and add a revalidation period to update them in the background.

- We can prebuild static paths for each page using the generateStaticParams() function in Next.js so they are ready to deploy ahead of time.

- We can improve caching by deploying to a service such as Vercel – this caches at the edge, improving performance based on where we source content. At the same time, we should be mindful of only serving the assets needed for each locale, such as specific font files.

Naturally, what we do will depend on your specific circumstances – for example, if your customers want English as their default but live somewhere like Scandinavia. We might not need to worry too much about optimizing for their region if we have already done it for English! Leaving that aside for a moment, let me walk you through what we could do to help optimize our localized content – for this demo, I'm assuming you want to use SSG or ISR (Incremental Static Regeneration).

WALKTHROUGH – USING ISR/SSG TO OPTIMIZE LANGUAGES

For this walkthrough, we'll be using the page.tsx file, in the \app\ [locale] folder:

1. Crack open the file in your editor – scroll down to the bottom.

2. At the bottom, leave a line blank, then add this generateStaticParams() function:

```
// Pre-generate pages for all supported locales
export async function generateStaticParams() {
  return [
    { locale: 'en' },
    { locale: 'nl' },
    { locale: 'fr' }
  ];
}
```

3. Leave a line blank, then add this constant:

```
// Enable ISR: revalidate page every 60 seconds
export const revalidate = 60;
```

4. Save the file and close.

At this point, I would typically say to restart the server so the changes take effect, but given we're working locally, I'm not sure how much of a gain we would see! Leaving that aside, though, I suspect there is one thing on your mind: Are these changes all we need to optimize our content?

Breaking Apart the Walkthrough

The short answer to that last question is potentially yes! There is a proviso, though, so let me explain.

The two options we've used, generateStaticParams() and revalidate, are key features of Next's App Router, which help with page rendering and caching on our site.

The first, generateStaticParams(), tells Next.js which locale pages to generate and pre-render during the build process – in our case, we're looking for pages for EN, NL, and FR markets:

```
export async function generateStaticParams() {
  return [
    { locale: 'en' },
    { locale: 'nl' },
    { locale: 'fr' }
  ];
}
```

If we had added others, these would also be included. We also have the revalidate const, which tells Next to regenerate pages after a set period – however, this is only if the content has changed. This is a great reason Next.js is so helpful with VSO – it handles a lot of this process for us automatically, as long as we provide enough information for it to do so.

Okay, let's crack on: we've added a lot of code, but there is one process we've not touched on. How do we test everything? We ran a visual test earlier, but this won't be enough; we must perform proper testing! Let's fix that now by diving in and looking at what sort of unit tests we can run; I'll also touch on what we could do in terms of broader testing.

Testing the Changes

Testing, testing ….123 ….

Okay, this isn't the sound test for some concert, but something a little more down to earth!

Testing, as I'm sure you can appreciate, is an essential part of any feature development; given that we're now using voice, this can make testing harder as we have to allow for constraints such as regional dialects and the like. To give you a flavor of some of the challenges you are likely to face, I've listed some below, which could trip us up if we don't allow for them:

- Testing supported languages: do we have sufficient support?

- How do we test SEO to validate the tags that we add?

- Mocking content: is it enough to include content in the tests, or is the preference to mock content from a JSON file? Also, what happens if content changes – can we write tests that validate the markup, irrespective of what content we use? Should we even be testing content?

- Can we simulate any accents, dialects, and regional variations that could be misinterpreted?

213

- We need to check formats for items such as dates and currencies: are they rendering as expected?

- We need to make sure dynamic URLs match what we expect: if we have specific URLs we want to test against, do we set up a shared data source so all tests for this feature use the same data source? At the same time, we need to be mindful of whether we should mock content or work because we test functionality only and not specific content.

Just a few to think about! This is why it will be key to get people who are native speakers of our target languages to be part of the testing. We can deal with some of the more straightforward tests where we check for the presence of certain words or tags, but if we're testing spoken content, then it will help to have native speakers available.

Okay, let's set that aside and focus on writing some code! Writing tests for this functionality could (almost) fill a book in its own right, so we'll focus on setting up the basics for our test suite before adding some sample tests.

USING CYPRESS TO TEST LOCALIZATION – PART 1: SETUP OF CYPRESS

I've chosen to use Cypress for this demo as it's my favorite. It works well with NextJS, although it will require us to run the demo site in a separate window while we run the tests.

Please feel free to use something like React-Testing-Library or Jest – this demo aims to show the principles of what we need to do rather than the specifics of how we execute it!

To get Cypress installed and configured, follow these steps:

1. First, we need to install Cypress – for this, crack open a Node.
    js terminal session, then change the working folder to our
    project area.

2. At the prompt, enter npm i cypress

    --save-dev, and press Enter to start the process.

3. Once completed, enter npx cypress open at the prompt, and
    press Enter to open Cypress.

4. When Cypress opens, click Enter to get past the welcome notes.

5. Next, choose E2E testing (Not Configured).

6. For front-end framework (Next.js detected), hit Next step.

7. On the Install dev dependencies screen, hit Continue.

8. On the Configuration files page, click Continue.

9. Wait for it to initialize the configuration, then choose Chrome as
    the preferred browser.

10. Hit Start E2E Testing in Chrome.

At this point, we don't need Cypress's GUI open – we will run the tests
via the command line. We still had to run through steps 4 to 10, though, as
this configures Cypress (to an extent) in the background. Now we have it
running, let's switch to adding our test.

USING CYPRESS TO TEST LOCALIZATION – PART 2: RUNNING THE TEST

To add a sample test, run through these steps:

1. First, go ahead and create a new folder called e2e under
   \cypress.

2. Next, crack open cypress.config.js, and replace the e2e
   block with this:

```
e2e: {
  baseUrl: "http://localhost:3000",
  env: {
    languages: ["en", "nl", "fr"],
    // Supported languages
  },
  setupNodeEvents(on, config) {
    return config;
  },
},
```

3. Next, crack open a new file and add this code – this will be our
   sample test. We'll start with a bit of pre-config:

```
describe("Multilingual Site Tests", () => {
  const languages = Cypress.env("languages");
  // Retrieve languages from config

  languages.forEach((lang) => {
    context(`Testing ${lang} version`, () => {
      beforeEach(() => {
        cy.visit(`/${lang}`);
      });
```

4. This next block performs a check for specific text in the
    Switcher component:

```
it(`Checks correct language content is displayed for
${lang}`, () => {
  const contentMap = {
    en: "Search Posts",
    nl: "Zoek Berichten",
    fr: "Rechercher des Articles",
  };

  cy.contains(contentMap[lang]).should("be.visible");
});
```

5. In this block, we test to see what happens when we click the
    French button:

```
        it(`Tests navigation to another
        language`, () => {
          cy.get(".language-switcher").within(() => {
            cy.contains("Français").click(); // Example:
            switching to French
          });

          cy.url().should("include", "/fr");
          cy.contains("Bienvenue").should("be.visible");
        });
      });
    });
  });
```

6. Save and close all files.

7. Next, we need to get our site running and ready for the tests
    to work. Fire up a second Node.js terminal, then change the
    working folder to our project area.

8. Enter npm run dev in the second window, and press Enter.

9. Next, switch to the first Node.js terminal, then at the prompt,
    enter npx cypress run and press Enter.

10. Wait for the tests to run through – if all is well, we should see
    output such as this appear:

```
Running: multilanguage.cy.js                    (1 of 1)
  Multilingual Site Tests
    Testing en version
      √ Checks correct language content is displayed
        for en (1680ms)
      √ Tests navigation to another language (1778ms)
    Testing nl version
      √ Checks correct language content is displayed
        for nl (1555ms)
      √ Tests navigation to another language (1716ms)
    Testing fr version
      √ Checks correct language content is displayed
        for fr (1423ms)
      √ Tests navigation to another language (1340ms)

  6 passing (10s)
```

11. The tests are now complete – we can close everything.

You may see this error appear:

```
Missing baseUrl in compilerOptions.
tsconfig-paths will be skipped
```

Don't worry! It won't affect the tests, but fixing it going forward would be good. My research shows this may be a challenge, as it needs changes to baseUrl, which conflicts with existing settings.

Excellent – we now have some limited testing in place, so we are ready to expand into a complete suite at a later point. We've covered some valuable points in this last demo, so let's look at the changes we made in more detail and explore some areas where we can expand testing of this functionality later in development.

Breaking Apart the Code Changes

I must confess something at this point – I suspect my choice of test suite could be very polarizing!

Before anyone gets into a war of words, I will point out that most test suites (at least the ones I work with) are very similar – indeed, Cypress wraps Jest in it, so if you wanted to use Jest on its own, the tests would work just as well. It is up to personal choice or existing requirements, depending on what you may or may not already have in place.

That aside, I elected to keep this demo relatively simple to get us going and show that we can add more once the basics are in place. We began by installing Cypress using the standard npm install process before launching it and running through the configuration process. Although we would not use the GUI, it was still necessary as it performs several tasks in the background, such as adding the fixtures and support folders containing files necessary for Cypress to operate.

In part two, we added an `e2e` block in the Cypress configuration file – this tells Cypress which languages we want to support and provides a value for `baseUrl`, which points to the root of our site. Next, we started to add the test; the first part ran through a bit of pre-config for visiting each locale. We then check that a specific label is present in each locale before clicking the French button to ensure we can switch to a different locale (using French as the locale). We wrapped up the test file and then fired up a terminal session to run through the tests and verify a successful result.

Working with Stakeholders

Okay, we've done the easy part. Here comes the tricky work: stakeholders!

While some people may think I have something against them (and before you ask – I don't!), we must be mindful that stakeholders can be finicky about what they want. I know from experience that some may ask for something flashy and glamorous, but implementing it will create a massive headache – a perfect example being icons that need to load on desktop and mobile. If these icons look fabulous but are enormous (say 120Kb), we must strike a workable compromise to get them down to a sixth of that size while maintaining the glitz and glamor!

However, stakeholders are not limited to those in management – we have to deal with others outside of the immediate development team who have a stake in the site. It might range from those providing content to colleagues who deal with SEO and product owners for the site but who have to answer to senior individuals! Everyone has a part to play – the tasks we need to look at fall mainly into three separate areas:

- Language considerations
- Business Processes
- User Experience Design

Let's have a look at each in more detail, beginning with Language.

Phase 1: Language Considerations

This phase details the language aspects, covering such aspects as providing the right translated text for each locale, ensuring text includes nuances for each market, and using the right keywords for SEO purposes. I've outlined some example areas and tasks to explore in Table 5-5.

Table 5-5. *Language considerations*

Topic	Tasks
Multilingual Voice Feedback	Provide audio responses in the user's preferred language using text-to-speech (TTS) APIs Consider nuances in tone and phrasing for different cultures
Voice Search Keywords	Research long-tail keywords and phrases users commonly speak in each language Adapt SEO strategies to account for natural language queries
Cultural Sensitivity	Adapt phrasing and examples to match cultural norms, avoiding idioms or phrases that may not translate well
Inclusive Design	Support languages used by minority groups in target regions Avoid assumptions about user preferences based on region alone

This is one area where having access to a native speaker will help – it could be the difference between a complex, risky job and a walk in the park!

Phase 2: Updating Business Processes

In this phase, we look at business processes, covering such aspects as compliance with data handling and privacy and maintaining up-to-date translations. I've outlined more examples to explore in Table 5-6.

Table 5-6. *Updating business processes*

Topic	Tasks
Data Handling and Privacy	Ensure each site complies with regional privacy laws (such as GDPR), and we provide transparency about voice data storage and usage
Language-Specific Data Models	Train voice models with language-specific datasets Continuously update models to include emerging trends and terms How do we keep on top of language/cultural changes?
Continuous Localization	Use tools like Crowdin or Lokalise to manage translations efficiently Implement a feedback loop to improve translations and functionality over time

For the first two phases, it might be worth exploring the use of AI and ChatGPT to help formulate content, such as translations or a data privacy template. If we go down this route, I would recommend using it to create a generic starting point, then work on specifics away from ChatGPT so we don't expose anything sensitive!

Phase 3: Updating the User Experience Design

For this phase, we cover some of the tasks that our UX team will need to look at – given these all focus on design, I'll list them below:

- Do we need to adjust for different text directions, such as Arabic or Chinese?

- Use culturally appropriate symbols – the more we can use universal symbols across multiple languages, the easier it will be, but this should not be at the expense of causing any issue!

- Be mindful of any instance where language differences can affect the width of elements, such as buttons or navigation. A great example is English vs. German – labels in German are nearly always longer and ultimately skew the design!

- Ensure that we have the right assets in place, such as fonts and icons – the former may be easier to source if we can use prebuilt ones, such as Roboto or Open Sans, but icons could be more complicated. At the same time, we need to consider the user experience – if we click a microphone button, for example, what should happen?

- Check all UX designs to ensure any extra elements (such as microphone buttons) fit existing designs and not make them too cluttered or busy. If the latter becomes an issue, we might have to adapt the design to reposition elements or use an alternative mechanism to help keep it clean and straightforward for customers.

- Consider the customer journey, particularly where we might need extra feedback, such as turning the microphone on or off, displaying a label when the microphone is active, and transcribing any spoken input.

I'm sure there will be more things to consider! Implementing speech, and in particular, as part of VSO, is still relatively new; many of the basics, such as GDPR and UX designing, still apply, though, so as long as we keep conversations happening, then we should be able to bring everything together, keep it maintained and compliant once we implement our project into production!

Summary

Going international is a big step for any site – we can cater to markets outside our home country in pretty much any language we want to support! It takes a fair bit of configuration to get the basics in place – over these last few pages, we saw how to do this, so let's take a moment to review what we have learned.

We began way back by looking at the different areas we need to cover when it comes to going international – we saw that there is a fair amount to cover and that we have to prioritize it all! We then moved on to build a demo to see how internationalization works. We ran through this process in stages; we learned that it isn't always easy to divide the work into sensible tranches and be able to test all of them individually. It's for this reason that we split up the work, but we had to postpone the testing until we completed the final part of the construction.

With the demo in place, we switched to the key part, which is adding international voice support. We created a button to control the microphone, learned how to configure the Speech API, and hooked it into the demo so we could control the search by voice.

Moving on, we then looked at optimizing performance. We walked through this as we're running our demo locally, so we wouldn't benefit until we upload it onto a remote domain. We then created some basic tests to verify that the correct labels were displayed and that we could switch between locales; we explored some ways to expand the testing as part of further development.

To finish things off, we examined the most critical part of the development process – working with stakeholders. We touched on how stakeholders can be choosy and that we must balance keeping the glitz and glamor they may want, the functionality we need for customers, and maintaining sensible architectural and technical limits in our projects.

Phew, we have come to the end of our adventure! I've had a great time building and writing this book – it's had its ups and downs while highlighting that Svelte is still a relatively new technology with a few quirks. But hey, all frameworks create their little quirks over time; it's just a case of learning how to get around them to achieve your desired result. I hope you've enjoyed the content and found something helpful, as much as I have, and that you can put it to good use in your future projects.

Index

A

A/B testing, 42
Accessibility, 13, 17, 25, 34–37, 43, 52, 53, 55, 90, 93–101, 165
aHrefs site, 16
AI, 18–20, 42, 43, 99, 145, 147–149, 156–159, 174, 222
AI-driven analytics tools, 19
App Router option, 163
App Router structure, 163

B

Beta testing, 134

C

CDNs, *see* Content delivery networks (CDNs)
Change prioritization
    advanced features and compliance, 165–167
    checklist, 163
    enhancing user experience task list, 165
    foundation task list, 164
Chatbot, 147, 148, 157, 158
ChatGPT, 101, 148, 149, 153, 155, 222

ChatResponse component, 155
Chrome's Lighthouse tool, 52
CNA, *see* Create-next-app (CNA)
Code reusability, 209
Constants, 78, 81, 136, 138, 150, 185, 188, 200, 211
Content delivery networks (CDNs), 29, 60, 62
Create-next-app (CNA), 169, 170, 172
Cypress, 214–220

D, E

dangerouslysetInnerHTML tag, 81, 82, 139, 140
Demo development
    adding remaining files, 188–190
    adding search facility, 183–187
    assumptions, 168
    breaking into parts, 182
    committing changes, 191
    Emmanuel Efavero's demo functionality, 168
    exploring challenges, 195–197
    implementing *basic* language support, 173–175
    LanguageSwitcher, 187, 188

© Alex Libby 2025
A. Libby, *Beginning Voice Search Optimization*, Design Thinking,
https://doi.org/10.1007/979-8-8688-1841-7

Demo development (*cont.*)

POC, 168–172

POC steps, 176–181

scaffolding, 172, 173

search box, 167

testing, 191–194

Design

accessibility, 34–37

analytics, 37–39

assembling the team, 26–27

challenges, VSO and
accessibility, 36

developer tasks, 28–32

framework assessment, 22–25

stakeholder engagement, 39–41

UX experience, 32–33

Developer tasks, 28–32

Development process, 23, 33, 39,
66, 101, 225

Dialect and conversational
speech, 167

F

FAQ, *see* Frequently asked
question (FAQ)

Featured snippets, 2, 13, 74–77, 101

Feedback, UX, 33

Fetch data, 24

Frequently asked question (FAQ),
36, 76, 133, 145, 146, 148,
155, 166

G

generateMetadata method, 182

generateMetadata() function, 196

generateStaticParams() function,
210, 212

Geolocation, 143, 209

Google, 81

devices, 134

featured snippets, 30

voice search, 3

Google Cloud Speech-to-Text, 197

Google's Rich Results Test
facility, 137

H

handleSearch event handler,
119, 188

handleSearch() function, 129

Home() function, 136, 182

HTML elements, 139

HTML Web Speech API, 147

HTML5 Web Speech API, 107,
108, 148

Hummingbird and BERT
algorithm, 11

I

Image optimization

Apress site, 65

changes to the demo site

W, X, Y, Z